The Business of Life

An "Inside-Out" Approach to Building a More Successful Financial Planning Practice

By Michael F. Kay, CFP®

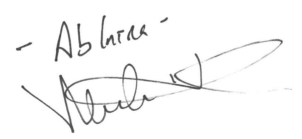

The Business of Life
An "Inside-Out" Approach To Building
A Successful Financial Planning Practice

AdvisorPress
>   www.advisorpress.com
>   1153 Bordeaux Drive, Suite 109
>   Sunnyvale, CA 94089
>   info@advisorpress.com
>   (408) 400-0400

ISBN 10: 1-60353-021-5

ISBN 13: 978-1-60353-021-7

$34.95

Printed in the United States of America.

Advance Praise for Michael Kay and *The Business of Life*

"With *The Business of Life*, Michael Kay has provided financial advisors who want to be life planners in the deepest sense with a wonderful road map, from a practitioner who has truly learned to 'walk his talk.' Practical and inspiring both. A real contribution to a newly emerging field."

~ **Olivia Mellan,** Speaker/Author *The Client Connection* and *Money Harmony;* Psychotherapist; Money Coach

"A practical, actionable guide to developing better, deeper financial planning relationships with your clients."

~ **Joel Bruckenstein, CFP®,** Co-publisher/Producer, *Technology Tools for Today* newsletter and annual T3 Conference

"Michael Kay is a strong voice in the financial Life Planning movement who clearly understands the life-altering potential of this powerful new approach to financial advice."

~ **George Kinder, CFP®, RLP®,** Founder, The Kinder Institute of Life Planning; Author *The Seven Stages of Money Maturity®* and Co-author *Lighting the Torch*

"This book provides a comprehensive template for a young financial planner to get it right, from the beginning—personally and professionally—and cut out years of reinventing oneself along the way. More importantly, Michael's work provides a step-by-step guide for planners to experience the power of financial Life Planning firsthand, so they can more effectively integrate the process into their work with clients."

~ **Joe Pitzl, CFP®,** Founder, Intelligent Financial Strategies; President, FPA NexGen 2010

"Michael Kay presents a unique perspective not just on the concepts of Life Planning, but on the process to transition your existing practice to integrate more of a Life Planning approach. Replete with wisdom from Michael's own experiences in making this 'quant-to-life-planner' journey as a veteran CPA and financial planner, this book is a must-read if you are considering a new direction for your own work with clients."

~ **Michael E. Kitces, MSFS, MTAX, CFP®, CLU, ChFC;** Publisher, *The Kitces Report;* Director of Research, Pinnacle Advisory Group

"*The Business of Life* is marvelous! Michael Kay has done a remarkable job of demystifying financial Life Planning, and what it means to call oneself a financial life planner. This is the first book to explain in plain English (well, New Jersey English, anyway) and in great detail what financial Life Planning is, how it deepens and enriches the planning process, how (and why) he does it, the steps and nuances of each phase, and how to develop competence and comfort as a financial life planner. Michael is clearly a master practitioner but more than that, he is a masterful teacher— for his clients, the members of his firm, and his readers. By presenting a clear and sound framework, detailed case examples, useful insights about creating a successful practice, and candid discussion of his own journey from finance professional to financial life planner, he brings clarity and eloquence to an arena where confusion and misunderstanding are in too great supply. *The Business of Life* is made-to-order for those who have asked 'What is financial Life Planning about?' Reading it, you will find dozens of moments in which you hear yourself saying, 'Oh, now I get it.' This is the right book, at just the right time. I'm proud of Michael for this masterwork."

~ **Edward Jacobson, Ph.D.,** Author *Appreciative Moments* and
Working Appreciatively

"Any financial advisor who is trying to strengthen client relationships will benefit from reading *The Business of Life.* Michael Kay has done a masterful job explaining how Life Planning has enriched his life and the lives of his clients. If you are looking for 'a track to run on' in your practice, I recommend Michael's book to you."

~ **Alan Werba,** Chairman of the Board, Loring Ward Advisor Services

"Michael Kay combines wit and wisdom to tell a very engaging story—his own personal journey from success to significance. And, in the process, he lays out a clear framework and action plan for all financial planners who want to forge stronger and deeper relationships with their clients and to build practices that will thrive in all market conditions. This is a book for our times—a clarion call."

~ **Carol Anderson, M.S.,** President and CEO, Money Quotient®; Co-author
Your Clients for Life

"A must-read for financial advisors who want to make a profound difference to accelerate the growth and health of their clients' lives. Michael clearly defines a process by which all financial advisors may effectively help their clients achieve their dreams. His 'inside out' approach turns the financial advisor table around from a focus on money to becoming a better listener, gain greater understanding and build deeper relationships with clients which engenders an ever increasing trust between advisor and client. Kay's argument for continual change is a beacon of hope for advisors stuck in neutral spinning their wheels in frustration and confusion resulting in a powerless state of being."

~ **Gary Klaben, ChFC,** President, Coyle Asset Management Company;
Author *Changing The Conversation*

"Michael Kay's personal storytelling style makes his book a comfortable read, and the exercises he includes are useful and clear. This would be an excellent resource for any financial planner who wants to add interior services to a practice but isn't sure where to start."

~ **Rick Kahler, CFP®, MS, ChFC, CCIM,** President, Kahler Financial Group; Co-author *Conscious Finance* and *Wired for Wealth*

"With his customary wit and humor, Michael provides an insightful blueprint for creating a meaningful and effective financial Life Planning practice. *The Business of Life* is a valuable read for any planner looking to improve his business and the quality of his life."

~ **Jeff Wheeler, JD,** President, The Wealth Collaborative

"Michael is deeply committed to transforming the lives of his clients through Financial Life Planning. His book will give you the content and the courage to do the same for your own firm and your clients!"

~ **Louis Barajas, CFP®,** Author *My $treet Money* and *Small Business, Big Life*

"What a breath of fresh air this book is—and so on target. As a financial planning professional of over 23 years, I too have come to the conclusion that Life Planning should be the core process we take our clients through, to ensure their financial success, and more importantly, their happiness in life. It takes a truly enlightened individual to not only recognize this, but to employ it in their own life and in their client process. Bravo Michael!"

~ **Karen J. Lee, CFP®, CLU, ChFC,** Founder, Karen Lee & Associates, LLC; Author *It's Just Money*

"A must-read for financial planners and staff who really want to take their practice to the next level! Many in the industry say that if we want to be taken seriously we need to develop into a profession (like doctors, attorneys and accountants). The Life Planning process that author Michael Kay outlines in *The Business of Life* will definitely elevate our industry into a profession. I would also recommend that students graduating from financial planning undergraduate programs read this book. It will help provide them with the communication and listening skills many graduates lack."

~ **Gary D. Davis, Jr.,** President, Beneficial Concepts Group

"Author Michael Kay has taken a close and serious look at the one model for financial planning that simultaneously brings joy and fulfillment to BOTH the client and the advisor. This will be a must-read for present and future generations of financial advisors who believe that the only success worth having is one that acknowledges their own values and needs along with those of their clients."

> ~ **David J. Drucker, MBA, CFP®,** President, Drucker Knowledge Systems; Co-publisher/Producer, *Technology Tools for Today* newsletter and annual T3 Conference

"A thoroughly enjoyable read! Michael Kay does a masterful job telling his own story—from miserable/overworked number cruncher to happy/healthy financial life planner—while continually inspiring the reader (yes, you can do this, too!) and laying down a clear and scenic pathway for 'inside-out' success. *The Business of Life* is a great contribution to the financial planning profession. I am very proud to call Michael Kay both client and friend."

> ~ **Marie Swift,** President and CEO, Impact Communications; Author forthcoming book *Become a Media Magnet*

"Michael Kay's new book is a long needed addition to the 'How To' library for financial planners who want to be the best. The step-by-step process he details is, to my way of thinking, how financial planning has always been done by the best planners—long before someone coined the phrase 'life planning.' In *The Business of Life*, Michael Kay gives advisors just the right amount of process and systems, mixed with the philosophy and spirit he brings to his practice. All the reader has to do is add knowledge, expertise and a passion to genuinely improve people's lives."

> ~ **Bud Elsea,** Bud Elsea Productions, Inc.; Former Director of Education, Financial Planning Association

"Advisors are always looking for an edge. Well, put this book on your desk and read it. Michael has nailed it! He has poignantly exposed the struggles of our vocation and gone one step further—helping us to design a better way."

> ~ **Diane MacPhee, CFP®,** Advisor Business Coach, DMac Consulting Services

Contents

Acknowledgements . . . . *i*

Foreword . . . . *v*

Introduction 1

Part One: Setting the Stage

Chapter One
What is Financial Life Planning? 9

Chapter Two
Client Communications 21

Chapter Three
Pre-contemplation: The Confines 35
of the Status Quo

Part Two: Inside

Chapter Four
Self-Inquiry: Where Am I? 47

Chapter Five
Exploring: Looking In and Looking Out 59

Chapter Six
Deciding: Folding or Going All In 63

Chapter Seven
Visioning: Beginning at the End 67

Chapter Eight
Positioning: The Transition 77
from Thought to Action

Part Three: Outside

Chapter Nine
Is it a Fit?. 95

Chapter Ten
Data Gathering 115

Chapter Eleven
Bringing the Plan to Life 133

Chapter Twelve
Presenting the Plan 149

Chapter Thirteen
Where the Rubber Meets the Road: 167
Implementing the Financial Life Plan

Chapter Fourteen
Monitoring and Completion 175

Epilogue 187

Appendixes

1. Individual Action Summary 191

2. Financial Satisfaction Survey 192

3. Wheel of Life Exercise 193

4. Money Memories Worksheet 194

5. Life Transition Survey 195

6. Visualize Your Future Worksheet 196

About the Author 197

Endnotes 199

Acknowledgements

In Chronological Order:

My Parents, both gone but not forgotten: Thank you for introducing me to the world of music and a love of learning.

Al Roth, the butcher and my first boss: He showed me that it is all about how you treat people. He treated all his customers with respect and treated a thirteen year old me like a person.

Me: for memorializing in the 9th grade that some day, I would write a book.

Carmine Fornurato, trumpet player with the NY Philharmonic and my first REAL trumpet teacher: The first person to introduce me to that rarified area outside of my comfort zone.

Rick Hyne: He's always there when I need him, just not always when I want him. He is a constant reminder that drive, dedication and commitment are mandatory for success. He also proved to me that I possess a certain ability to persuade, regardless of his inability to throw a straight ball from short to first.

Wendy Titlebaum (now Kay): Who, in college, introduced me to the idea of love and support and has stood with me through all the ups and downs. She possesses strengths and abilities that I don't. She is the love of my life and best friend. She also makes great kids. It's been a long time since our first talk in the common room in Earle Hall.

Gordon Asnis, CPA (deceased): For convincing me that I could be a great accountant.

Arthur Hodes, my friend and mentor: For helping me see that being a great accountant wasn't all that great and that possibilities existed beyond my imagination. He never doubted my ability, drive or passion (and if he did, he never told me!) I cannot thank him enough for all his help and support all these years.

Ron Howard: Who introduced me to passive management and LoringWard, chocolate molten lava cake and roller-blading in Santa Monica. He also led me to my first "A-ha!" and helped usher me out of my comfort zone.

Marty Kurtz: Who opened my eyes to the fact that there are forward-thinking professionals who care deeply about their lives, businesses and clients. He has graciously and generously shared his knowledge and helped aim me in the right direction.

Benjamin Yudin: For introducing me to the concept of being present, being intentional and just "being."

P. Alan Loss, Leslie Kelly, Charlotte Hartmann-Hanson, Jeff Shoffer, Kay Confer, Bobby Glass and the rest of the original **East Coast CFO Forum:** They brought their knowledge, experience and vulnerability and challenged our beliefs in order to make us all better.

Jack Fersko: A voice of reason, wisdom and heart. He is a model of what it means to lead with dignity and clarity. His depth of intellect and compassion makes him a constant inspiration to me.

Michael Gerber: His talk was a giant wake-up call and his seminal work has been a constant companion in my thinking. He is the originator of my second "'A-ha!"

Metro Duda, Olga Raykhelson, Patrice Nicita: The original members of Financial Focus. You guys believed in me and still do! Thank you.

Dick Zalack, president of Focus Four: For his incredible work that helped me see my life beyond my work. His methods and coaching helped guide my thinking and still do.

Carol Anderson: Her work opened me up to a process that changed my life, yet again. She is an inspiration and has supported my efforts throughout the writing of this work.

Hugues Rivard, Charlie Weidman, Kathy Molinaro, Ashley Fox, Patrick Brydon and **Bill Timpson,** the newest members of the Financial Focus family: All believers in helping clients and living a balanced life. You guys believe in me too! Right?

George Kinder: His books and workshop helped me look inside and confront my truths. His insights and knowledge are the foundation of our great profession.

Misty Fuentes: Without her help and inspiration, this project would never have happened. She helped me develop the concepts for this book, did the research and helped me believe that I could do this, even when I didn't.

Angela Zusman, my editor and friend: For her guidance, strength and confidence in my ability to put words on the page with meaning, clarity and passion. Without her extraordinary patience and determination, I don't see how I could have finished. She has a tough job!

Louis Barajas: For generously giving his time, sharing his vision and doing so with a full heart. He is among the best of us.

Industry thought-leaders **Rick Kahler, Ben Coombs** and [Coach] **Ed Jacobson:** Whose insights, experience and willingness to speak the truth make them special.

Marie Swift and her **Impact Communications Team:** I acknowledge their great talent for taking something "raw and unfinished" and working diligently and patiently, making slow and steady improvements. Can't wait to see what we'll do together to rock the world once the book's in hand!

Joe Pitzl, a leader in the FPA NexGen community: I so appreciate his taking the time to read this work, but most of all appreciate Joe taking a leadership role in the next (and presumably better) generation of financial advisors.

To all the pioneers, leaders, educators and writers who have worked so diligently and honestly to help make our profession one that helps clients live a more balanced and valuable life: I honor their experience (you know who you are!).

Peter Johnson at Advisor Press: His willingness to bring my work into reality is much appreciated. He also disproved the idea that publishers suck.

Bob Veres, a great luminary in the financial planning world: Bob has done so much to support the life planning community. I'm so grateful to Bob for his generosity in writing the foreword to this book!

To my children, **Elyssa** and **Mitchel,** and my newly acquired son, **Dave.** They keep me young, make me laugh, make me think, and give me hope for the future of society.

Foreword

Almost everything you read and hear (books, articles, webinars, speeches, newsletters) about practice management, client services and life planning was created by people who are not actually doing these things in their own practice. You read the advice of Susan Galvan, Mitch Anthony, George Kinder and Carol Anderson (and, sometimes, me) on life planning; Mark Tibergien, Philip Palaveev and Chip Roame offering practice management tips; writers, editors and journalists in our various trade magazines providing expert opinions—and what is often missing from this tide of information is that reality check that comes from a practitioner who has struggled to put theory into practice.

It sounds great. Does it actually work? Will it work the first time, or are there hidden obstacles that nobody told me about, because they didn't actually experience the process of implementing the idea into the day-to-day routine of an advisory firm?

Reading Michael Kay's book, it quickly became clear that he believes much of what I do about where the profession is going and how to get there. You can state these almost as theorems:

- Life planning—that is, a deeper exploratory process that helps advisors understand and address a person's most cherished goals—is becoming an essential part of the delivery of financial advice.

- You cannot offer life planning services effectively without applying its principles to your own life and practice.

- Becoming a truly effective financial planner is a long and often trial-and-error struggle toward better procedures and a fuller understanding of the possibilities of the service itself.

- Much of the trial-and-error can be circumvented by learning from somebody who has made the mistakes and gone through a difficult evolution, and is willing to share the best practices he/she has learned along the way.

- You will be different from anybody you take advice from, so this advice becomes more valuable if the advisor also shares some systematic approaches that allow you to fit what he/she has learned into your own framework and comfort zone.

What you have here, in this book, is a concentrated, organized version of the often-haphazard advice you get in the hallways of FPA conferences. Michael Kay offers you a comprehensive look at his journey toward better client service and personal effectiveness, what he learned along the way, and a lot of helpful processes by which you can customize his experiences to your own practice.

Everything you read here has been tested in an actual working, successful advisory practice. The book talks about what it feels like to present a financial plan and discover that it doesn't include something vitally important to your clients. You read about the common situation where clients never look at your numbers—or, worse, when you present the numbers and then realize that your client's eyes have long since glazed over.

In some cases—as in Chapter Eight, when clients refuse to answer the Kinder questions and stop your life planning process in its tracks, or the real-world check in Chapter Ten that states in plain English that just because clients can envision something impossible doesn't mean you should encourage it—you get the real world answer to questions that are impossible to answer by anybody who hasn't applied the theory to living human beings.

Whether we know it or not, we are all moving toward a future where you've taken control of your life and practice and applied the same principles that got you there to helping your clients do the same. We all move at different speeds, and we all have our own challenges in terms of time, inclination and access to good information. This book, *The Business of Life,* was created to help you accelerate your pace and move past some of the hidden obstacles that are in your way. It may also help you move toward that future with clearer vision. Because it speaks from the practical world of the practicing advisor, you can give the things you read here a bit more trust than the many words written and spoken by non-practitioner "experts."

You're on the road and the future is waiting. Michael Kay's wish—and mine—is that this book will take some of the struggle out of your journey into a better life offering better client service.

Bob Veres
Editor and Publisher, *Inside Information*
Columnist, *Financial Planning* magazine

Introduction

"Ab Intra"

(From Within)

"Michael, there's a call for you on line 1, also Mr. Austin is holding on 2. Your 10:00 appointment is waiting in the conference room and don't forget to sign those applications and letters before you go to lunch. Oh, and don't forget you promised to finish the plan for Dr. Katz before the end of the week. You're meeting on Monday!"

"Lunch? What lunch?"

"You're meeting Mr. Samson and his CPA at noon at the sushi restaurant."

"I am?" It was thirty degrees below zero outside. Who wants sushi? I wanted a bowl of chicken soup and a bag to hide my head in.

That's what my life was like, day in, day out; a constant cram of phone calls, meetings, appointments, plans and correspondences. I looked over my desk at the stacks of files my assistant tried her best to keep orderly. I noticed the stack of unread journals teetering on one corner and the ever-growing pile of unopened mail on the other. It was semi-controlled chaos. I tried to find order, but in truth I was totally overwhelmed. Lighter fluid and a match seemed like my only alternative.

At home, things weren't any better. I wasn't spending enough time with my wife or my children; I was woefully out of shape and my finances, although not a disaster, weren't getting the attention they deserved. My personal time was confined to the five-minute car ride between my home and my office. Even though I could be considered successful—after all, my business and income were both expanding every year—my business had overtaken my life to the extent that I felt out of touch with my career, my loved ones, and myself. Looking in the mirror, I wondered whose life I was living. How had this happened?

The truth is, this pattern had been building over the years. My daily life was a battle of love and hate. I loved being a financial advisor but hated the constant feelings of pressure, exhaustion and frustration. I loved the fact that this career could provide me with independence, joy and the opportunity to make a real difference in the lives of my clients, but I hated the fact that my own life was stressful and out of balance. This wasn't what I had imagined for myself or worked so hard to achieve. How much money and how many new clients would it take before I would feel truly successful? Where was the freedom and joy?

Even more frustrating, though, was the feeling that I could be doing a better job for my clients. While I was technically competent and certainly cared deeply, something was missing. My focus and performance were inconsistent. Sometimes, the plans I created were a perfect fit for my clients and other times they were met with indifference or worse. Too often I was not hitting the target, which was not satisfactory for my clients or myself. I knew that there had to be a better way. My experience couldn't be the apex of financial planning, especially given the stress and anxiety I brought home to my wife and children and the fact that I was scarily close to dropping dead from a heart attack. I wanted success, but at what cost? For the first time in my life, I truly felt afraid—which was a good thing. As we all know, fear can be a great motivator but for a while I was mired in this state of helplessness, perpetuating the same frustrating daily routine.

My moment of truth occurred in a most unusual and unexpected way. My wife and I—on one of our rare outings together—were shopping for the kids. She pulled an outfit off the rack and was turning it inside out. I asked what she was doing, and her reply initiated the chain of events that eventually lead to this book. "I turn the clothes inside out to examine the seams," she explained. "If they're not tight and sewn properly, the clothes will fall apart."

Wow! I froze. My mouth dropped open. My wife thought I was having a stroke but luckily it was only an epiphany. My internal seams were coming apart. It was time to turn myself inside out and check out what was *really* going on. I realized that I needed to recalibrate my focus from the life of business to the business of life.

How about you? How are you doing?

You are a financial planner. You have your own practice, or work within somebody else's practice. Maybe you're just learning the basics. Maybe you've been doing this so long you can't imagine not doing it. You may feel successful, or you may feel that success is just around the corner. Regardless of your situation, you must consider this question: What does success look like to you? Let me ask this a different way. Can you see your life as a whole? Are the components of your life everything you wish them to be? Are you physically and financially fit? How are your relationships with your friends and family? Do you have time for hobbies and personal growth? What makes your life full, rich, and remarkable?

The business of life involves much more than work and money. It is filled with all kinds of twists and turns that we expect ourselves, and our clients expect us, to successfully navigate. Some advisors do this with natural ease. Most of us, however, need a structure or process to help us collect all the relevant information before being able to discern the best path forward. What information, though, and when? As financial planners, we are taught how to collect the numbers—but when it comes to addressing our own lives and the needs of our clients, the numbers alone don't quite do it.

For financial planners in particular, the needs of our clients are becoming exponentially more complex. The numbers are easy to acquire but they just don't tell the whole story. In addition to the numbers, I've learned, we need to understand behaviors, habits and what motivates people (including ourselves) to live a fuller and richer life. Many planners have difficulty asking the tough questions, feeling it is too invasive or uncomfortable for them and for their clients. For this reason, they may not know their clients well enough to be able to help them make the decisions that are most closely aligned with their values and dreams. In addition, the state of our economy has many planners spending more and more time trying to get more clients; their own needs and the needs of their business become secondary. It's amazing how many "successful" people I meet who are exhausted by the endless race of keeping up the numbers. They are working for the numbers instead of letting the numbers work for them. I get it. That was my life too—until I developed a systematic approach to helping my clients clarify what is most important to them and then guiding them through life's transitions. Before I could help my clients, though, I had to help myself.

In the course of engaging with this book, you will have the opportunity to evaluate where you are with your own life and practice so that you can move forward in the direction that is ideal for you. Only then can you help your clients do the same.

This "inside out" approach to building a more successful practice results from many years of research and experience. My own "inside out" process resulted in a migration from quant-based planning to a more balanced combination of quant and life-planning approaches. I will describe this transition in more detail in the coming chapters; for now, suffice it to say that I am a believer. I believe in the benefits of Financial Life Planning[1] because of how this methodology has enriched my life, improved my practice and helped my clients make greater progress in living their dreams. For this reason, I believe it is my obligation to share what I've learned with more advisors who, in turn, can then reach more clients. It is my hope that this will have a long-term impact on helping our society live a more values-based life.

Many readers of this book are already practicing their own brand of life planning. I too used my own intuitive version of life planning before creating a distinct process. It worked fairly well but without a systematic process, there was no consistency or structure. For example, I didn't have the foundation of knowledge and research to know how to ask the right questions at the right time. I also had a harder time training successors and staff. This book is an attempt to present this systematic approach so you can clarify your own process and make the changes that best support your goals.

The first part of this book will take you through the process of examining your life, your business and your client relationships. The second part provides a step-by-step guide to transforming your practice to include a life planning approach so that both you and your clients will achieve new levels of success—specifically, success that brings true satisfaction and joy. The goal of this book is to help you recognize that not only is positive change possible, it is essential to experiencing true success. With this awareness and understanding, you will gain the ability to help your clients do the same. For this reason, as you work through this book, you will be putting yourself through the same processes you'll later utilize with your clients.

Throughout the book there are exercises, examples, dialogues and suggestions to assist in your process. The book follows a step-by-step approach, therefore, I suggest that you do not skip from chapter to chapter until you've read the book through first. After completing the book, it should be used as a reference and each chapter can stand on its own to assist you in reinforcing your progress.

I've never thought of myself as a "writer." Still, I want to help others benefit from the great material I've discovered in my years of study and practice. As a result of the exercises and tips in this book, I am a much happier, healthier and therefore more successful human being. My practice is thriving, as is my personal life. Yes, I discovered, you can have it all! It will require some effort; it will require a willingness to look inside; but you may be pleasantly surprised by what you find there. I invite you to join me on this great adventure to discover your true potential as a financial advisor and to bring that excellence to your clients and the world. Now *that's* success!

Part One:
Setting the Stage

Chapter One

What is Financial Life Planning?

"Every new beginning comes from some other beginning's end."

~ Seneca

Sitting in the back of an expansive conference hall, I listened intently to the academic explain to the advisors in the room that all the hysteria concerning the "Great Recession" shouldn't freak them out. He had an awesome array of charts, graphs, and data to back him up, and his performance was dazzling! Like myself, the other advisors in the room had looks of awe and relief on their faces. Then the conference ended and we all walked out, buzzing and excited about our new charts and information. When I got home, I reviewed the graphs and statistics we'd received as handouts. I thought about how I could use this information to actually help my clients … and the feeling of relief faded away.

I admit it right here and now—I can appreciate a good graph as well as the next guy. But I had to ask myself: will those charts seep into the hearts and minds of my clients and remove their doubts and fears? No! They're nifty tools, but they are not enough. A graph showing historical asset class returns since 1916, past recessions, standard deviations and allocation models is not going to help a client get through devastating markets. The game has changed. While this data is still relevant, none of it means a thing unless you connect with your clients on a far deeper level. In short, it's time to put "life" into the business of financial planning.

The concept of Financial Life Planning was developed by a group of advisors and academics who saw the need to utilize a holistic approach in working with their clients. While this idea may seem like an obvious direction, it represents a philosophical shift from the traditional quantitative approach. Quant-based planning does not fail the client or the practitioner. But as a practitioner who has integrated Life Planning into my personal life, my practice and my client relationships, I have lived the difference; so have my family, my colleagues and employees and most especially, my clients. It's like driving a Lamborghini instead of an Audi TT; they're both sports cars, but let's face it …

Life Planning, Financial Life Planning®,[2] Integrated Planning, Holistic Planning, Client-Centered Planning, Values-Based Financial Planning®[3]… all of these titles describe an attitude, approach and system of working with clients that goes beyond the numbers. Indeed, we can call it Financial Planning done correctly! After all, The CFP Board of Standards has enumerated in practice standards (100-1, 200-1 and 400-3)[4] that we, as CFPs, are required to define the scope of our engagement; determine a client's personal and financial goals, needs and priorities; and communicate our recommendations in a manner and to an extent reasonably necessary to assist the client in making an informed decision. It's all there, in black and white. While traditional financial planning, which I will refer to as a quantitative approach, relies more on numerical projection to determine the success of a plan, a Financial Life Planning model seeks to develop a more in-depth understanding of the client's needs, goals, values, dreams and priorities. The weakness—or limitation—in the quant-based approach is that when the data-mining is limited to numbers, performance, projection, simulation and analysis, essential (though less accessible) information is likely to be missed.

It wasn't very many years ago that I practiced traditional financial planning; after all, I am a CPA by background and was comfortable with numbers. My process was simple: meet with a client, ask them about their goals, gather the data, analyze the information, prepare and present a voluminous ream of paper that boiled down the goals to spreadsheets, charts and graphs. I was totally comfortable with this format, until I had to admit it just wasn't working.

I recall one case where we had done all the data collection, asked the questions regarding the clients' goals, checked their numbers with them and then presented a plan based on our analysis of their financial position. At the plan presentation meeting, where we shared our findings and made our recommendations, the clients displayed a great deal of discomfort. They began picking apart the numbers. Then they told us that they were no longer sure they agreed with the goals they had originally shared with us.

The meeting ended with the clients promising to get back to us once they checked their numbers and clarified their goals. They never did get back to us. In retrospect, I realized that after all my hard work, I still didn't really know my clients. I didn't know their dreams, their history, or their core values. I didn't know what they would need to increase their "pillow factor"—the ability to put your head on the pillow at night with a sense of comfort and ease. Because my questions and concerns centered on their numbers, I had not earned their trust. Earning trust is something I will discuss throughout this book, because it is foundational to every planner's success.

Where do financial planning and Financial Life Planning hit the fork in the road? As I've said, traditional financial planning is aimed at the quantitative approach to understanding a client through the numbers, while a Life Planning approach marries the numbers with a deep and considered knowledge and understanding of the clients' goals, needs, dreams and aspirations. The key word is *deep*. Many traditional planners have worked with their clients for many years and have a close relationship with them. They know all their client's family members' names and have a good understanding of where the client has been and where they want to go. This knowledge is great; yet ideally, it shouldn't take you many years to get to know your clients. The more quickly you get to know them on a *deep* level, the more effective you can be.

Having worked both ways, I can tell you without equivocation that the quality of the plans, the relationships and the outcomes are much more fulfilling, more accurate and more meaningful for all parties as a result of my implementation of life-planning processes. How can one truly define the engagement's scope unless you understand where the client is going and what they need and want out of the relationship? How can a planner and client mutually agree on goals, needs and priorities unless there is a deep knowledge of the client, their strengths, experiences, resources, limitations, background and history? How does a planner properly prepare and present a plan that truly captures the clients' goals, needs and priorities, unless the client is open, forthright and speaks without fear of judgment? In other words, without this knowledge, understanding and trust, the financial plan is a mathematical presentation of possibilities rather than a roadmap to the achievement of dreams.

The Foundation of Financial Life Planning

I am not alone in my beliefs, nor am I the first to articulate them. Back in 1995, George Kinder co-founded "The Nazrudin Project," a group of experienced financial advisors committed to exploring money and personal finance from the aspect of a more human and spiritual perspective. In 2000, Kinder published *The Seven Stages of Money Maturity,* a seminal work that expounds on the need for advisors and consumers to recognize that *a financial life includes more than money.*

In January 2001, Carol Anderson, educator, researcher and writer, founded an organization called Money Quotient with the goal of providing financial advisors and other professionals with the tools and training they need to assist their clients in developing a more successful and satisfying relationship with money. Money Quotient is focused on education, research and promoting a life-centered perspective to building client relationships and to delivering financial advice that is aligned with the unique set of values, priorities, and circumstances of the individuals and families being served. It was Money Quotient that trademarked the term Financial Life Planning, and the Money Quotient tools and training are instrumental in my life-planning methodology.

Later that year, in the *Journal of Financial Planning* (October 2001), Lewis J. Walker, CFP®, CIMC, CRC, declared: "The trend that will govern the future of the financial service industry is the fundamental shift from product to process." Walker went on to explain that the future of financial advice will be framed in a "holistic process aimed at the completion of life goals, our own and that of the client(s)." Similarly, Tracy Herman, a writer for *Registered Representative,* described the role of a contemporary financial advisor as a "Life Planning concierge with a wealth of resources."[5]

Having noted a growing interest among financial professionals in a more personal and holistic focus, the National Endowment for Financial Education (NEFE) in 2000 convened a think tank of pioneers in the Life Planning movement to explore this emerging trend. Collectively, this group of experts settled on a definition of Life Planning.

Life Planning is the process of:

- Helping people focus on the true values and motivations in their lives;

- Determining the goals and objectives they have as they see their lives develop; and

- Using these values, motivations, goals and objectives to guide the planning process and provide a framework for making choices and decisions in life that have financial and non-financial implications or consequences.[6]

Sounds good, right … but does it work? I can almost hear you saying, "Show me the numbers!" Finding and presenting quantitative data on the efficacy of Financial Life Planning is difficult for several reasons. First of all, it is a very new development, utilized by few practitioners. There is currently little or no standardization in the industry. Therefore, creating baselines of data is a significant challenge.

In 2006, members of the Life Planning Consortium (comprised of such industry notables as Carol Anderson; Deanna L. Sharp, PhD, CFP®; Susan Galvan, president of Galvanic Communications; Martin Siesta, CFP®, Compass Wealth Management, LLC; and Andrea White, MCC, president of Financial Conversations) developed and conducted "The Survey of Specific Elements of Communication that Affect Trust and Commitment in the Financial Planning Process." The FPA co-sponsored this research and the CFP Board of Standards, Inc., provided the funding.

After conducting the research, Anderson and Sharp analyzed the data and wrote up the results in a White Paper entitled "Research: Communications Issues in Life Planning: Defining Key Factors in Developing Successful Planner-Client Relationships," published by the FPA Press. Their goal was to "identify and statistically validate specific communication topics, tasks and skills that contribute to building client trust and commitment in the context of a professional financial planning relationship. In particular, we explored elements of communication that are associated with a Life Planning approach to service delivery. We also examined the influence of selected communication variables on important indicators of successful planner-client relationships including client retention, satisfaction, cooperation, openness, and referrals."

The study, abstracted in the *Journal of Financial Planning*, concluded that there is a growing interest in a holistic, client-centered, values-based approach to developing successful client relationships as the financial services profession evolves from transactional to consultative. Furthermore, the research found that today's clients demand more from the planning process than a packaged plan. As Sharp states, clients want an "empathetic understanding of their values, needs, goals and desires and the ability to integrate financial products and plans in ways that satisfy those values, needs, goals and desires."[7]

The study highlights the fact that the CFP Board of Standards, specifically 200-1, addresses the need for qualitative data gathering. This recommendation presents a significant challenge to those who have not employed a qualitative approach in understanding their clients' needs and goals. There is a gap in the knowledge bank for practitioners. They can go to school to learn about retirement planning, investment analysis and the other disciplines in financial planning; however, there is little in the way of formal curricula to learn qualitative methods. The study indicates that client trust and commitment were enhanced when utilizing a holistic, client-centered approach. Moreover, client retention, satisfaction, cooperation, openness and referrals were all positively affected.

The study provides some empirical data that supports these conclusions. In addition, there is an overwhelming amount of anecdotal information gleaned from practitioners who have integrated Financial Life Planning into their process, detailing how this integration has changed them, their practice and their relationship with their clients. As Jeff Wheeler, JD, President of The Wealth Collaborative, Inc. in Los Angeles, explained to me:

> *There is no shortage of books and articles on the topic of wealth … how to acquire it, how to invest it, how to leave it to heirs, etc … but little is written about the importance of wealth as a medium through which we express extremely important details to ourselves, and to others, about who we are, who and what we value and what we stand for. In the Life Planning process, we uncover those details and, in so doing, reveal ourselves, our passions and what we **truly** want from our lives and our money. Armed with and empowered by that knowledge, we then learn to harness the power of money in order to bring congruity between what we want and how we live … to create the life we want to live, as well as the person we wish to become. Life Planning has helped me, as well as my clients, get far more from their lives and their money than we could have ever achieved through portfolio management and financial planning alone. In my view, it's an utterly essential tool in the financial advisor's shed.*

Adding her personal perspective, Dianne H. Webster, CFP®, President of Integrated Financial Services, LLC, of Amesbury, MA, told me: "In addition to differentiating my business from other financial service organizations, implementing a Financial Life Planning process has significantly benefited my client relationships. By opening a conversation based on life concerns rather than financial concerns, the client is often better able to articulate his or her needs. Further, it helps me gain a deeper understanding of the client's motivations and priorities so the financial plan is fully relevant to the circumstances of the client and family. I have developed stronger and longer relationships with my valued clients, and as a result my work is more fulfilling. I go home at the end of each day feeling that I have helped make life better for my clients."

What does this information mean to you? Well, let's go back to what Lewis J. Walker said. He states that financial planning is a "holistic process aimed at the completion of life goals, our own and that of the client(s)." Notice that he included "our own" in the mix? This means that in order to successfully integrate Life Planning into your practice, you will first need to evaluate *your own* goals and see how they're being met, and then make any necessary changes. Only by looking inside can you comprehend what you truly want to change on the outside.

The "Inside-Out" Approach: What to expect from this book

You've heard the history and benefits of Financial Life Planning. I hope you are excited and motivated to implement life planning into your own work as a planner. So how do you get from here to there?

The "Inside-Out" Approach consists of eleven steps, each of which is described in detail in the following chapters. See the table below for a brief description of each step. The remainder of this book is a guide through each step of the process.

Name of Step	Description
Self-Inquiry	Look inside and assess your personal life, business, and finances
Exploring	Examine your answers to the self-inquiry questions to see where you are on track and where you'd like to make changes
Deciding	Review your answers and make decisions about how you will move forward. Seek advice and feedback from trusted colleagues about your ideas
Visioning	Looking ahead to your ideal future: in detail!

Positioning	Time to make some changes! Prepare yourself, your business and your clients for your new life-planning approach
Fit Meeting	Select the right clients for your business and introduce them to the life-planning approach
Data Gathering	Collect all the information you'll need—both qualitative and quantitative
Bringing the Plan to Life	Integrate all the qualitative and quantitative data and create a plan that addresses your clients' needs, dreams, and financial musts
Presenting the Plan	Create the ideal environment and present your client with their plan
Implementing the Plan	Outline specific actions that will keep your clients on the road to success
Monitoring	Support and motivate clients to stay on track

The "Inside-Out" Approach to Financial Life Planning begins, of course, on the inside—that is, inside *you*. As you examine the steps of the process, you will see that the initial steps are for the planner. Once the foundation has been laid, you are ready to take further steps within your business and with your clients. Your experience of introspection and the other steps in the process will shed light on your preferred direction. In addition, your experience of this internal process will help you guide your employees and clients along a path to their own preferred future. It's time to walk the talk.

Your level of success depends on your level of belief in the process as well as the amount of time you are willing to put into each step. To avoid feeling overwhelmed, I recommend you break the process down into small pieces performed over time instead of cramming all the steps into a few days. Use your calendar as an ally and create space in your day, week and month to actively work on change. Approach each of these meetings you set with yourself with the same level of importance as those you set with clients; if you put them off because you *can*, it will be very difficult to make headway. There's almost nothing easier than procrastination and the great excuses that go with it. One doesn't lose a pound of excess weight by starting the diet tomorrow. You must be doggedly determined to bring positive changes to your life and business.

Dealing with Change

As you go through this process, I earnestly hope and expect you will change your approach to financial planning for the benefit of all. The basic definition of change is to become or make different. But how does change happen? In 1977, James O. Prochaska of the University of Rhode Island and his colleagues began to formulate a model of change. Twenty years later, they concluded that change is a process involving progress through a series of six stages.[8]

1. **Pre-contemplation:** the stage before change that occurs before the individual is even aware that change is needed or desirable

2. **Contemplation:** a period of self-evaluation that motivates and directs future actions

3. **Preparation:** the individual believes they can change, is committed to change, and creates the conditions conducive for change

4. **Action:** the act of change, such as creating modifications in one's lifestyle

5. **Maintenance:** continuing actions that prevent relapse, such as positive reinforcement and ongoing support

6. In some iterations of the model there is a final stage called **termination,** in which the individual's actions have ensured that the change is final and permanent

Prochaska's model is a helpful guide to the process of change that we go through in changing our life and business and that our clients go through in making changes in their lives and their relationship to money. This structure is useful for financial planners in particular for a few reasons. First of all, most financial planners I know are very adept at processing data and *loooove* systems. Second, change can be less daunting when it is broken down into smaller pieces. Third, change requires motivation, and nothing motivates us better than progress. With this model, you can gauge where you are in your process and have clarity moving forward. Finally, this model will also help you understand and guide your clients to modify their negative financial tendencies.

We are incredibly fortunate to be in a profession that helps people live their dreams while we work to live ours. It is incredibly rich, meaningful and rewarding, and it is best approached with a sense of gratitude for those who have paved the way for us to walk a smoother path. The field of financial planning will continue to grow, evolve and improve as planners raise their game and clients' needs increase in our ever more demanding lives. Together, we can add to the knowledge base and continue to improve, grow and evolve.

My goal is not to create lines of division in our wonderful profession, but to challenge each of us to think beyond our collective comfort zones. I remember sitting in a meeting with some of my colleagues several years ago as the moderator Ron Howard shouted, "No learning takes place in the comfort zone! No growth takes place in the comfort zone! You must break free of that place to achieve greatness! It isn't comfortable or easy, but it is necessary if you wish to break through to the next level of success!" At the time I just wished he'd stop shouting. Now, I am shouting the same thing. For the super talented and successful traditional planners, I throw down the gauntlet of challenge! It isn't that traditional planning doesn't work. It's just that by adapting a more holistic approach to planning, you can reach new heights of success, for the benefit of all. As you move through this book, you will find many opportunities to look inside your life and your practice and discover what changes will allow you to be even more successful than you already are, and then guide your staff and clients to do the same. The point of this learning and growth is to improve our lives and our businesses and to help our clients live their dreams. You've already embraced business. Now it's time to look at your life and set the course for the future of your dreams. Enjoy!

Chapter Two

Client Communications

"The single biggest problem in communication is the illusion that it has taken place."

~ George Bernard Shaw

Question: How do you eat an elephant?

Answer: One bite at a time!

Integrating Life Planning into your practice is definitely a bite-by-bite affair, detailed in Part Two of this book. At the same time, it might be easier than you think. As professionals, we all know the steps of financial planning, from discovery to implementation and monitoring. They are fundamental to our work as planners and clearly defined by the CFP® Board of Standards:

1. **Establishing and defining the planner-client relationship**—The financial planner should clearly explain or document the services to be provided to the client and defines responsibilities of both parties. The planner should explain fully how he will be paid and by whom. The planner and client should agree on how long the professional relationship should last and on how decisions will be made.

2. **Gathering Client Data, including goals**—The financial planner asks for information about the client's financial situation. The planner and client mutually define personal and financial goals, understand time frame for results and discuss, if relevant, the client's attitude about risk. The financial planner gathers all the necessary documents before giving any advice.

3. **Analyzing and evaluating the data**—The financial planner should analyze information to assess the client's current situation and determine what must be done to meet the stated goals. Depending on what services are required and agreed upon, this could include analyzing your assets, liabilities and cash flow, current insurance coverage, investments or tax strategies.

4. **Developing and Presenting the Plan**—The financial planner should offer financial planning recommendations that address a client's goals, based on the information provided. The planner reviews and explains the recommendations to the client to help them understand them so that informed decisions can be made. The planner should also listen to all concerns and revise the recommendations as appropriate.

5. **Implementing the Plan**—The planner and client must agree on how the recommendations will be implemented. The planner may provide the needed solutions in alignment with the recommendations or serve as "coach," coordinating the whole process with the client and other professionals such as attorneys or stockbrokers.

6. **Monitoring the Plan**—The client and the planner must agree on who will monitor your progress towards your goals. If the planner is in charge of the process, the plan needs to be reviewed periodically and report to the client periodically to review your situation and adjust the recommendations, if needed, as your life changes.[9]

If you review the preceding list of the financial planning process, it is easy to see that Life Planning does not supplant or subvert the financial planning process: it enhances it! Life Planning doesn't replace technical analysis, spreadsheets and mathematical calculations. It just helps define the goals more clearly, creating better communication and trust. Not only do you get to keep your beloved Monte Carlo simulations and remain in the hunt for Alpha, but you are able to use what you've learned from your clients to feel confident that your work has meaning. Gone will be the days when you question the validity of your work. Life Planning will help ensure that there is no "disconnect" between the work you are doing and what the client cares most about.

Integrating Life Planning into your process allows you to move into territory that has, until now, been the domain of a very special few. Many clients have told me after experiencing a life-planning meeting that they never expected to feel so comfortable or to so easily share their personal thoughts and experiences. We all have our private fears, mistakes, misjudgments, and dreams that we keep locked away, sometimes not even shared with our spouses or those closest to us. Later in this book, you will read about a couple that discovered more about each other during this process than they could ever have imagined.

I believe most people are eager to pop the cork on their fears, wishes and dreams but are too afraid of judgment or reproach. In this case, it's possible that your technical knowledge and abilities will mean exactly zip unless you can integrate them with a clear and deep understanding of your client's true goals, dreams and needs.

It's not always easy to get this information. I appreciate the ogre in Shrek who talks about ogres being like onions—complicated, with lots of layers. Well, as you've undoubtedly discovered, it's not just ogres who have layers. In my clients and in myself, I've seen layers of fear, doubt, greed, overwhelm, enthusiasm, love and confusion, amongst many other emotions. There's one's personal history to consider, as well as how that history impacts their life today. A perfect example is the client who grew up during the Depression or is a child of parents of the Depression—fear of another Depression is imbued in their thinking and thus, decisions about money are centered around that fear. The same can be said of someone with a money history where there was a lack of valuation around money, and they have become profligate spenders. No financial plan, unless there are unlimited resources, is going to be successful if there is unrestricted spending. It is an invitation to failure. Where do your technical abilities leave you if you are unable to access this information? Only at the outermost layer.

How does one peel back the layers? The planner cannot find out what needs to be known unless the client opens that door. The key to that lock is *trust*—not the trust that you are technically competent and can create dazzling flowcharts and lay out the perfect investment allocation. Rather, it is the trust that you understand who they are and what they care about; a trust that you are not sitting in judgment and that they, while imperfect and flawed, have value and worth, and that their dreams and goals are important and worthy of attainment. People do not like feeling incompetent, especially about money. For some strange reason, there is generally little embarrassment when people are unable to fix their plumbing, but when it comes to money, there is a great deal of consternation when there is a lack of understanding and control.

The key to opening the lock is trust. And the key to trust is communication. When communication is free and open, the conversation flows effortlessly. How can you ensure free and open communication? The essential elements of successful communication, while basic and obvious, are not necessarily easy or natural to consistently manifest. Here are a few practices to help keep your communication successful.

1. Do what you say you're going to do—consistently.

2. Listen more than you talk, and listen fully and actively.

3. Be aware that people process information differently from one another.

4. Think before you speak.

5. Speak and act in a non-judgmental manner.

6. Ask questions.

7. Be direct.

8. Remember and understand why you're there.

9. Provide your clients with a sense of control over the process.

10. Be respectful.

1. Do what you say you're going to do—consistently.

This sounds like the most basic, simple and easy thing in the world, right? Well, it is. But somehow, we don't always do it consistently! Have you ever said one thing and done another? Hey, we're only human. However, when it comes to working with clients, any disconnect between what you say and do can be a fatal blow in establishing trust. After all, why should a client trust you? Another client may have referred you, or you might have met them on the golf course, but there has been no bond of trust built yet. Trust takes time, care and diligence.

During meetings with clients, I am careful to record our tasks and those expected of clients on a form we call the Individual Action Summary (see appendix). Keeping a record helps delineate and remind everyone about what has been said and agreed to. Before the next meeting, I go over the list and ensure that all my action points are complete. When we meet again and I've completed my action points, I have created a small but invaluable experience of trust that not only binds me closer to my client but also motivates them to perform their tasks. If your clients cannot trust you to do what you say—all of the time—the chance of building trust is negligible.

2. Listen more than you talk, and listen fully and actively.

Yes, you've heard this a billion times. But how often do you actually do it?

Listening fully and actively begins with intention. It just isn't natural for most of us to listen. We're much more comfortable spilling forth our knowledge, understanding, experience, insight or humorous anecdotes about our children. Perhaps this works when you're talking to your mother, but hear me loud and clear: Most clients assume your technical competence—that's not their big issue. You perform your technical wizardry when they've left the meeting room. When you are with your clients, what they want to experience is your ability to hear them, understand them and help them. They are thinking not about you but about their own universe of worries, cares, problems, successes and accomplishments. No matter how big it is, there just isn't enough space in your conference room for you to step into the spotlight. That doesn't mean you should be mute, just muted. No matter how much they like you, they are not in your office to hear about you: so keep your stuff out of your clients' time.

While we are on the subject of listening, let's talk about active listening. When I was younger, I mastered the art of appearing to pay attention to others when actually I was basking in the brilliance of my own thoughts. I thought this was a laudable skill ... until I realized that I was totally missing the point of communication: to hear and be heard. Listening actively is not hard to understand—it is an extension of the Golden Rule, for we all want to be heard. But it can be rather tricky to do, especially on a consistent basis. It is, however, an art that can be learned and practiced. There are many books published on the subject, for example, *Listening: The Forgotten Skill: A Self-Teaching Guide* by Madelyn Burley-Allen.

Listening fully and actively begins with your intention. In order to listen actively, one must eliminate external (cell phones) and internal (what's for lunch?) distractions. Focus on how you are sitting (facing the client, sitting up straight, leaning slightly forward), make eye contact and think about what the client is saying, how they are saying it and what their body language is telling you. If the client doesn't believe you are hearing them, they are less likely to feel trust and open further. Be forewarned: The door shuts quickly and completely when they do not feel that they have been heard!

I'd like to suggest an exercise. At the next possible opportunity, enter into a conversation where your goal is to listen deeply and completely. With intention, listen to what is being said, the level of conviction, as well as the importance placed on the subject by the speaker. Make eye contact. Do not interrupt, even if you have just thought of the most hysterical or intelligent comment of your life. Once there is a pause, ask any clarifying questions that seem appropriate at the moment, such as, "Tell me more," or "How did you feel about that?"— or something that demonstrates your desire to know more. Notice if the energy of the speaker shifts as you engage with them. Once you have completed the conversation, think about what you witnessed and heard. What would your life—and your practice—be like if you listened actively all the time?

When I first started to consciously practice active listening, I tried it out on strangers. (God forbid people who knew me should get used to my full attention!) One day, in the checkout line of a grocery store, I called the checkout person by the name that was displayed on her nametag. "Wow, Mary, it seems like you're really busy today. How do you stay on your feet and deal with the craziness?" Her response was surprising. "Thank you for using my name," she said. "I am a person, even though most people never talk to me or look at me, and I feel as though I am invisible most of the time. And yes, it's been a busy day, but that's normal. Ever since I moved here from California six months ago, I've had to get used to such a different pace. Things are so much slower out there." She beamed. It was a really beautiful sight.

Getting chatty with a grocery store checkout person might not seem especially meaningful, but I learned a lot from that brief encounter. I learned that she feels invisible, she's had a life transition and that she's adjusting to a new and faster-paced lifestyle. Can you translate that experience into a conversation with a potential client and what you might possibly learn, if only you'd ask the right questions and listen to the answers? Unfortunately, some of us were trained to think that the way to a client's trust and confidence is to show them how smart we are. Well, guess what? The fact that the client is sitting in your conference rooms indicates that they believe you are technically competent; you now need to prove how well you hear and understand their goals, dreams and fears. Not only will this approach help your business, it's a wonderful and rewarding experience to truly connect with the people around you.

3. Be aware that people process information differently from one another.

As we discussed earlier, active listening is both verbal and nonverbal; in fact, communication is mostly nonverbal. It is your job to not only read your clients' nonverbal cues but also to figure out whether your clients learn best via verbal, visual or kinesthetic communication. Sorry, you can't ask a prospective client, "Would you like sugar in your coffee? And hey, what kind of learner are you?" Some clients can hear your words and understand what you're saying (verbal), while others need to see it in writing (visual). Kinesthetic learners need to hold something, touch something or see something happening. They need a sense of movement.

In a typical first meeting, our conference table is stocked with pads, pens, crayons (and chocolate!); the white board is clean and ready. As I talk through a point, I will *say it, write it* on the board and *use my hands or an object* (such as a brochure) to explain my point. I watch closely to see where the spark of understanding comes from and present my ideas in the most effective manner throughout the meeting. Being aware of your clients' learning style is extremely important in establishing trust and getting the most out your meetings. You are showing your clients that you know how to communicate effectively without ever having to ask awkward and difficult-to-answer questions about which kind of learners they are. You are also ensuring that they will retain more useful information, saving everyone a lot of confusion, frustration, and time.

4. Think before you speak.

I could put this suggestion in HUGE CAPITAL LETTERS! Perhaps you've had the opportunity to learn this lesson the hard way. Well, here's a chance to practice it before having to extract your foot from your mouth.

Thinking before speaking is not just about the words that you say. I've noticed several "experts" who, when asked a question, practically trip over their tongue to get the words out. Sometimes they even interrupt the questioner mid-question in their haste to appear wise. Here's a little tip: People will think you're smarter if you pause a moment or two to consider the question, fully and deeply. Before answering, ask yourself the following questions:

- What was the question?

- Do I fully understand what is being asked?

- Is there more to the question?

- Is there anything behind the question?

- Are there any clarifying questions I need to ask *before* I answer?

Once you have gone through this mental checklist and you are confident of your answer, consider how your questioner will best receive your answer. Ready? Aim! Fire! is so much better than Ready! Fire! Aim!

If you are not confident of your ability to answer a question fully, then announce just that. I've always been impressed when people answer that they need to do more research or time to consider before answering, or even admit that they don't know. You want to be honest as well as brilliant.

5. Speak and act in a non-judgmental manner.

Have you ever experienced a time when someone spoke to you like you were the dumbest person in the universe? It's amazing how quickly one can go from feeling like a Master of the Universe to a total schlump. When clients set foot in your office, you, as Master of the Universe, have the duty to help them feel decidedly un-schlumpy. One of the best ways to do this is to listen, speak and act without judgment. When your clients experience that you are not judging their lack of knowledge, their past or present failures and their lack of net worth, you have a much better chance of breaking through to the promised land of knowledge, trust and a deeply meaningful and long-lasting relationship.

One way to assure that you are judgment-free is to mentally prepare yourself for each meeting. (We will talk more about this concept in future chapters.) Once you are with your clients, it is essential that you are aware of your body posture. For example, having your arms folded across your chest is not an open posture, while using your hands with the palms open is welcoming. Your voice is also a very powerful instrument—not just the words you use, but the tone, timbre and volume are important elements in how you are perceived. Your words can say one thing, but if your tone, posture and attitude outshout your words, you create confusion and leave your client with a sense of being judged, sabotaging your efforts to build a solid relationship.

6. Ask questions.

This idea goes hand in hand with "Listen more than you talk." Asking questions for clarification shows the client that you are really trying to understand them. Have you ever had an experience when you went to a doctor's office, filled out the requisite forms and then, when the doctor finally came into the examination room, he or she said, "Good morning," glanced briefly at your chart and just blasted into the physical exam? Now, can you compare that to an experience when the physician looked at the chart and asked questions in order to understand you and your current situation in a deeper, more meaningful manner? Which experience made you feel more comfortable? Which doctor would you prefer to visit again?

Along with the idea of asking questions, craft questions that are open-ended, rather than asking "yes/no" questions. Create questions that dig to the heart or essence of what you need to know—questions that show you really want to understand. For example, I will often say things like "Tell me more," "What issues or challenges do you foresee?" or "What has your experience been in that area?" These are very simple questions, yet they open the door to greater understanding and demonstrate very clearly that you are interested in fully understanding your clients' specific situation.

7. Be direct.

This concept can be a lot trickier than it sounds. Of course you want to be clear, concise and to the point. You are the expert, the guru, the leader and guide for your clients, yet you walk a fine line. No one wants to be bullied or pushed; no one wants an advisor who doesn't advise; and no one wants to work with someone without the courage to be honest. The truth is the truth. Announcing the "elephant in the room" takes courage and conviction, and it is your job. Learning how to do so with respect and lack of judgment is a skill that you must practice. When you can do this successfully, your clients will love and respect you. Even if the medicine tastes bad, they will appreciate your commitment to their success. If a client does not want honesty and directness, the relationship you are building will always be less than sturdy. Is this kind of relationship worth devoting precious time and energy to?

A little caveat—I work in the New York area, where speaking directly is sometimes taken to its extreme. Those of you who are not from the New York metropolitan area might not feel as comfortable speaking this way. Start small and start slowly. Unlike what you might experience in New York, being direct doesn't necessarily mean being rude. Being direct means being honest, without burying the truth in piles of unnecessary verbiage that diminish the clarity and power of what you are trying to say. I believe anything said with kindness, non-judgment and authority can help move mountains and inspire action.

8. Remember and understand why you're there.

In day-to-day life we, as advisors, are constantly living under a multitude of challenges, pressures and problems. We have pressures at home to deal with—time pressures, money pressures, relationship and family pressures—while trying to fit living into life. As business owners, we have pressures from many directions: staff issues, overhead to cover and a business to build. In addition, we have the lives and successes of our clients and their families in our hands. Could there be a greater responsibility? Sometimes the burdens can seem insurmountable. This is where Life Planning becomes *who you are* and not *what you do*. In other words, being a life planner means that you strive to increase satisfaction and balance in your life too. Your ability to live a balanced, focused and directed life is vastly important, because it will provide you with the tools to feel at ease with your life and to be a living example for those whom you guide. The "Do as I say and not as I do" axiom just doesn't cut it here.

In order for you to bring your best to your clients, you must find your own clarity and peace. That means not walking into a client meeting thinking about the bills you have to pay or your daughter's soccer game later that day. It means knowing that in order to be successful, you must be open, honest, focused and directed toward the success of your clients. You must bring nothing but the best of you into each meeting.

I remember once walking into a client meeting when I was not in a good place mentally. I was feeling lousy, experiencing some personal issues that had my head spinning. I should have cancelled the meeting. Instead, I tried to fake it. I tried to get through the meeting wearing a mask of confidence and focus. My client saw through it almost immediately and said, quite firmly, "Michael, are you ok? You don't seem yourself." I explained to the client that I felt like I was coming down with something that had hit me suddenly. We cut the meeting short and rescheduled for the following week. I dodged a bullet, but only by being dishonest. This taught me a very clear lesson and was the last time I walked into a client meeting without being properly focused and ready. Remember, clients need consistency, and any deviation can be enough to throw all your hard work into the dumpster. Be mindful of the reason why you are doing what you do. You are playing a small part in a far larger play.

9. Provide your clients with a sense of control over the process.

Control is like a dance in the ways that it is given, taken and shared. When a client first meets with an advisor, they might be fearful because they do not know what to expect. They might be wary and suspicious, especially if their experience of working with financial professionals has been unsatisfying. They might even be willing to walk in and throw their keys on the table and say, "It's yours, drive it away!" giving up all control immediately.

Since you cannot know what you do not know, you need to create a process to understand your clients well enough to know where they need and want control, and where you as the planner should hold on tightly. Some clients wish to control the process to a very high degree—that is, until they have gained sufficient trust to loosen the reins. Others wish only to be told what to do and when to do it. The tricky part is understanding what your client needs and how to most effectively help them. If you are too forceful, you will scare them and they will be suspicious—not a good method for building trust. A successful planner knows when to take—and when to cede—control. When clients feel that they are being rushed, pushed or bullied into making decisions, they rarely follow through, and your relationship with them suffers. Yet, if you are too passive, they will feel that you are not guiding them, and they will feel equally uncomfortable.

In my practice, we spend a good deal of time talking about expectations. This conversation will take you a long way in gaining understanding with your clients. If their expectations are outside of your comfort zone, it is your job to communicate that clearly and definitively.

I remember a potential client who was referred by an attorney whom I'd worked with in the past. The client wanted me to invest his retirement plan assets. I asked him what he expected from me in our relationship; without blinking he told me that he expected me to call him three times a week to update him on his portfolio. (I don't know about you, but I wouldn't do that for my mother!) It's just not what I do and it made no sense to me, especially since the same information was accessible online. I thought about his comment for a moment and told him that while I would like to help him, his expectation was far beyond what was reasonable. I explained why I felt the way I did and said that I was sorry, but we would have to end our meeting. He sat, dumbfounded, and after considering my words for several minutes, said that he would like to work with me. He asked me what amount of time seemed reasonable to me for touching base. In the end, his concern wasn't based on a need to talk to me about his account balances and tri-weekly performance; it was about control. If I had acquiesced, he would have continued to create unreasonable expectations, and I have no doubt that eventually the relationship would have failed.

Providing clients with a sense of control begins at our very first meeting. I explain to potential clients that the timing of our planning process will be dictated by the speed and accuracy of the information with which they provide us. I offer suggestions, but they dictate how often we come together for goal setting, planning and implementation meetings. They tell us what is most important to them and in what order they prefer to address their concerns and issues. This process allows the client to feel ownership, safety and a sense that the advisor hears and respects what is most important to them.

10. Be respectful.

Of course, you are respectful. You have good manners and treat people with kindness and courtesy. You may even have clients that you hold in very high esteem. This is fantastic ... but let's go a step further. Asking for help might be difficult for your clients. Do you appreciate the courage that it took them to call your office and walk through your door? Do you understand that your frames of reference might be totally and completely different from theirs? Can you truly respect that their experiences, history and points of view might be foreign to you?

The person sitting in front of you is looking to you for help in achieving nothing less than their dreams and goals. Can you respect their personal journey of tragedies, challenges and triumphs? Recall for a moment a recent meeting with a new client. Take a moment and contemplate their journey, challenges and accomplishments. What has brought them into your life? What are you experiencing? Can you see a different dimension to your client? Can you see a shift in your attitude? Respect all clients equally. Don't reserve your respect for those whose behavior, values and accomplishments most closely match your own.

Building client trust is dependent on consistently excellent communication, and these ten steps are essential to that goal. Mastering the art of communication requires ongoing attention, awareness and practice. Even after years of practice, I still review these ten points before client meetings, because they remind me to be present and aware of what I wish to bring with me into each experience with the client. Remember, each and every meeting is an opportunity to strengthen or lessen the trust you need to deeply understand your clients. Without this understanding, your ability to help them will be mediocre at best; at worst, the time and energy you've invested will ultimately be for naught.

Chapter Three
Pre-contemplation: The Confines of the Status Quo

"To be conscious that you are ignorant
is a great step to knowledge."

~ Benjamin Disraeli

The first stage in the Prochaska Transtheoretical Change Model is called "Pre-contemplation," which literally means "before thought." It is that period when the idea of change is not present in our thoughts or consideration; when, in fact, one is so busy that the thought of adding one more item to the mental agenda feels like being asked to climb Mt. Everest in the dead of winter—naked. The overriding quality of this stage is resistance, a sense that if it ain't broke, don't fix it! And what would you fix? At this point, you are just trying to maintain the status quo: pay the bills, meet all regulatory requirements, prospect new clients, get to the gym, attend back-to-school night. The thought of changing anything can be daunting, to say the least.

Yet, maintaining the status quo is not always in your best interest. In fact, it can be downright dangerous. As Langenberg's 29th Law states: If you don't know that you don't know what you don't know (or you don't care), you're a liability, and the degree of damage you'll cause is exponential to your level of power. So how do you figure out what you don't know?

The objective of this chapter is to provide a peek behind my personal curtain to see what life was like before I transitioned my practice into a life-planning model. I want you to share in my failures, missteps and frustrations as well as in the victories. This chapter offers an opportunity to see how my life, business and relationships with clients have improved as I plotted the course of my career and transitioned my business into a more holistic, client-centered practice. Perhaps some of this will sound familiar.

I started my professional career as an accountant and CPA in 1976. I readily admit that I was a musician hiding in an accountant's body, having faced the reality that Jon Faddis, at age eighteen, was already a billion times the trumpet player I would ever be. Hence, I decided to spend my days as "Mr. Debit the Door and Credit the Window Accountant." I aimed my attention towards the tangible world of numbers. I was fortunate to be exposed to a wide variety of businesses, industries, owners, controllers and clients, as well as to a wide spectrum of experience in the accounting world, from the intensely interesting to the most mundane: SEC Audits, 1040 preparation, bankruptcy audits, divorce litigation support, and financial accounting for businesses and professional practices.

Did I know numbers? Did I know analysis? You bet! The silent musical world of numbers was my sweet spot and comfort zone, the place where I grew up in the financial world. I could pull a financial statement and tax return apart and put it back together blindfolded. In short order, I transitioned from Junior Accountant to Manager, working my way toward partnership. My ultimate vision of myself was Michael Kay the CPA. After all, being a CPA and a partner in a successful practice wasn't anything to sneeze at—accountants are highly respected, professional and steady. There wasn't the even the faintest clue that my life would take a sharp turn off into another career. I mean, who spends four years earning a degree, working, getting a CPA license (no easy task) and building a practice to chuck it all away?

Nine tax seasons later, however, I did just that. My exit was precipitated by the cajoling and encouragement of my friend and mentor Art

Hodes. Art owns a successful financial services firm in central New Jersey. (I call it South Jersey, but he insists to this day that it's really mid-state.) He fervently believed that I would be "perfect" in this business and could transfer my skills directly into his firm, where a CPA would command respect and approach the sale of financial products from a more "learned" position. Once I completed a battery of tests and exams, I would be officially welcomed into the world of financial services, with my very own Rep Code and everything. Art was and is a firm believer in life insurance and could sell ice to the Eskimos, and do it on the back of a cocktail napkin. I say that with all love and respect; there is not a trace of slick or dishonesty about him. He speaks from his heart and soul and his true belief in protecting children and spouses from the disaster of death. There is no one I trust more.

My entry into financial services was fairly uneventful, until I found out that in order to make a living, I had to actually sell something. This was nothing like creating analyses, understanding the financial guts of a business or doing battle with the IRS. My job was to find people and sell them life and disability insurance, provide mutual funds or other suitable investments, and help guide them to make financially responsible decisions. For this, I would receive a commission on all sales. Sounded good! Yet it felt very felt awkward to me. Even though I knew in my heart and soul that I was acting in my clients' best interests, I still felt that there was an inherent conflict of interest. But there wasn't much time to ponder this dilemma. My wife had just given birth to our second child, and he was hungry! That gnawing feeling in my gut foreshadowed the anxiety and frustration that would be my life for the next ten years.

Working with clients, to me, was no longer an advisory relationship, but one in which I tried to convince them that they needed my products. I didn't realize then that people didn't want a product. What they wanted was to live their lives without worry. I began to create analyses to back up my rationale for making recommendations. My accounting experience began to creep back into my thinking and process. As time went on, I finally realized that I just wasn't comfortable with my life and business model. But this was the decision I made, and I had a family to support; there was no part of me that could sit and look squarely at my situation.

After all, what was more important—my business and family, or my slippery feelings?

Several years passed in this manner, some very good in terms of compensation and some very lean. I wasn't yet ready to get off the rollercoaster, so I moved it closer to my home by opening my own office just a few blocks away. While I was building up my list of clients, I was also trying my best to follow through with my promise to be there for those to whom I sold a product. The problem with this model, of course, is that it takes time to add clients, taking away from your time with the existing ones. I was stretched beyond my limit by my attempt to manage all the expectations of my clients, which meant doing everything from fielding phone calls, handling problems, prospecting for new clients, filing, and writing correspondence. I held the titles of CEO, COO, CIO and CFO. I even watered the suffering plants. It was too much! I lived in dread of clients calling and adding another "to-do" to my list. I was working six or seven days a week and averaging twelve hour days; the idea of a vacation was as far away as the beaches on the brochures my wife had by now stopped showing me. Man, I missed tax season; it was only four months long— this grueling routine was constant! I lived in dread of January 1st, because whatever I had done the year before meant nothing, and I was starting a new year at zero. I had to find new "pocketbooks" in order to create new income. While I loved the idea of helping people and the "freedom" of being self-employed, I was increasingly anxious, frustrated, exhausted and unhappy. I was beginning to wonder if I even wanted to be successful if this was what life would be like.

It was at this time, in 1995, that a saying from my childhood came to mind: "Why do you hit your head against the wall? Because it feels so good when you stop!" It was time to get my priorities straight and investigate new ways of doing business. Not long after that, I came across an article in a financial journal about creating a fee-based model. I dug a little deeper, talked to some associates, obtained some recommendations. This was my first big "A-ha". It lead to me create my own RIA and partner with a fee-based asset management firm whose fee-based business model was based on Nobel Prize-winning research by top academics from around the country. It was a win-win: clients receive investment solutions and I receive recurring income. No more dreaded January firsts!

In addition to helping me reframe my business model, the relationship paid immediate dividends by exposing me to great speakers such as Steve Moeller, Bill Bachrach and most importantly to the Dimensional Fund Advisors (DFA) model of investing. I was also invited to attend their first CFO Forum for East Coast advisors. The guest speaker was Michael Gerber, author of *The E-Myth*. This lecture was the hallowed ground of my second major A-ha!

The content of Gerber's talk was simple. He spoke about building a business "on purpose," about the need for systems, procedures, and a thoughtful approach to our work. He spoke about working *on* one's business rather than working *in* one's business. Working *in* your business is what we do every day: the calls, the meetings, the lunches, the analysis and all the tasks associated with serving clients and getting stuff done. Working *on* the business is so different. It is strategic rather than tactical. It means looking at the big picture and overall objectives, not the day-to-day routine. I realized that I had some possible control over the outcome of my efforts; for example, I am not a slave to my schedule but the maker of my schedule! I had heard these ideas before, but somehow, that day they resonated with me in a big way. The bells were ringing! I asked myself who I was at my best. The answer was simple: I am an advisor. It was time to move my business into a more advisory model. I continued to collect ideas and practices from respected sources. Even though I had a long way to go, I began experiencing renewed interest, enthusiasm and energy.

The next few years were devoted to conversion and growth. I continued to gain greater clarity and focus about my purpose. Through the CFO Forums, I met some incredibly insightful, experienced advisors, people like Marty Kurtz and Allan Loss—smart, caring and always willing to share their knowledge and experience. Every quarterly meeting brought more information, thoughts, knowledge and a clearer picture of my next step.

The new work model brought with it greater ease. I was better organized as my focus narrowed, cash flow was steadier and therefore easier to budget and plan, and I felt more at peace. My conversations with clients began to change as I introduced financial planning into the mix. The questions surrounding their futures, dreams and goals were the centerpiece of our meetings. Still, I knew internally that while I was on the path, I had not yet reached my goal.

By 2001, I was ready to build a financial planning firm with a team of talented professionals. We built our model around fee-based financial planning and a fee-based wealth management platform. Barely five weeks after the Twin Towers came down, Financial Focus, LLC, was born.

Our first years were basically spent recovering from the market collapse and the new world of post-World Trade Center terrorism and color-coded security alerts. Our clients were hurting from market losses and, while tempered somewhat by our investment model, they were still experiencing the fear, pain and insecurity that comes with each market-cycle downturn. We had plenty of missteps in everything from hiring to execution. We picked the wrong clients and we tried to say yes to everyone. Yet our concept was simple: help people by creating financial plans, use asset class investing to diversify risk, and be consultative.

Through my association with the management firm, I met Meir Statman, a professor of Finance at Santa Clara University, whose focus is on Behavioral Finance. Meir's words hit me like a brick and were as logical as gravity: people's behaviors were normal, which means basically irrational. I don't mean that in a pejorative sense, but the reality is, when markets are up, everyone wants to buy; when markets are down, everyone wants to sell. Not exactly prudent, but that's the way it goes. This knowledge of investor behavior impacted our thinking and our practice; as a result, we were better able to truly understand our clients and help them more effectively. It was also during this time that I met Dick Zalack, president of Focus Four, a coaching program for advisors and other business owners. This experience was to be yet another huge A-ha! for me and a guiding influence on the development of Financial Focus.

My associate and I committed to working with Dick through his three-year program, designed to help us work on our business and improve our personal lives while increasing our financial success. It was all about finding balance. We learned to take time away from work to "sharpen the saw," as Stephen Covey says.[10] We learned how to discern which of our activities brought the most joy and were most productive in terms of our financial goals. We learned to define ourselves and say yes to those clients who were a good fit and avoid taking on clients who weren't. We learned to accept the fact that our style was not for everyone. It was a meaningful step in our development, but I could feel that there was still a ways to go.

In 2005, at another CFO Forum, a friend and fellow advisor introduced Carol Anderson to the group. Carol, the president and founder of Money Quotient, talked about Financial Life Planning. It was the first time I had ever heard the term, and her presentation left me wanting to know more. Money Quotient, a non-profit organization, trains advisors to work with clients to build deeper, more meaningful relationships, to uncover their blocks to financial success and create conversations centered on their hopes, dreams and values. In February 2006, I attended my first Money Quotient training, which was the cherry on top of my A-ha! sundae. It put together all the pieces I had been collecting and added several I hadn't even known were missing. At this training, Carol introduced us to Prochaska's model of change, which provided a construct—and an explanation—for what my business and I were going through. I was mesmerized.

I also had an idea of what it would take to master the new skills. It wouldn't be the first time I was at the beginning of a long-term learning curve. This wasn't the kind of learning I could achieve just by reading books or attending classes. It would take, more than anything, persistence and practice, reminding me of my early days as a burgeoning musician. As a youngster, I'd always known what I wanted to be when I grew up: a professional trumpet player. I got my first trumpet and imagined myself making that shiny brass instrument burst forth with an amazing outpouring of sound that would make Doc Severinsen, Al Hirt and Louis Armstrong stand up and cheer. I listened to hours of recordings by Bunny Berigan, Bix Beiderbecke, Harry James, Fats Navarro, Dizzy Gillespie, and Miles Davis, imagining those life-altering sounds coming from my student Olds trumpet. The hours of lessons, practice, practice and more practice and blood, sweat and tears (playing like Lew Soloff of Blood,

Sweat and Tears was something I wanted desperately) earned me a level of progress—slowly, but progress nonetheless.

I remember one night when I was working through a particularly challenging exercise in the Arbans (the trumpet players' study bible). I flubbed and flopped, trying to get my fingers, breathing and rhythm synchronized. Over and over, I tried until I felt like kicking my music stand across the room. I just couldn't do it. I got up and walked away, ready to wrap my horn around the nearest pole. My dad walked downstairs to my room, stood in the doorway and saw the frustration on my face and my horn tossed onto my bed. My father was a Juilliard-trained string bass player. He could sing and play over two thousand songs from memory (a feat that still boggles my brain). He looked at me and said, "Mikey (to this day, he's one of only three people allowed to call me that), slow it down; make every sixteenth note into a quarter note, every eighth note into a half note and every quarter note into a whole note. Instead of trying to master this the way it's written, make believe it is way slower; then as your fingers adjust, you'll speed it up." With that bit of wisdom, he turned and walked out. I was both excited by his advice and irritated that I hadn't thought of it myself. I decided to give it a try. After a good deal more time and concentration, I got it. Not only did I get that exercise, I learned that there's more than one way to reach a goal, and that sometimes, the solution is to slow down.

So when it came time to change, I was both daunted and fortified. This change I was seeking would be much greater and more beneficial than the ability to play mediocre music, and look how much I had sacrificed for that! I wanted to be able to help my clients and myself to the best of my power, and I knew that mastering Financial Life Planning was the way to go. As Marty Kurtz, CFP®, President of The Planning Center, in Moline, Illinois, said to me:

> We know change is all around us, as a matter of fact, change is an integral part of our lives like breathing and eating. No one can avoid change. Financial Life Planning is the process of acknowledging our changing presence and determining what we control and don't control, what we influence and don't influence

and using those material facts, building a plan of action for the future. A plan that recognizes our values and ideals and builds mileposts (goals) along the way as we work toward those ideals. Financial Life Planning is framing work to create an authentic life, what a human needs to achieve true happiness. That is why I do Financial Life Planning and why I ask my clients to do it.

I'd like to stop here and give you a chance to challenge your brain a little. This is a warm-up for some of the exercises ahead that will take you through the process of change. I suggest you have some paper handy as well as enough time to really consider these questions without interruption.

Take a moment to think about a typical meeting with new prospects. Ask yourself the following questions:

1. Do I follow the same routine at every meeting?

   a. If so, how did I develop that system and how do I know it is as effective as it can be?

   b. If not, why not?

2. Do I evaluate what I could have done differently or what could have been done better?

   a. If so, what do I do with that information?

   b. If not, why not?

3. What was the last change I introduced into my process?

   a. Why did I make the change?

   b. How did I make the change?

   c. Is it now a consistent part of my process?

   d. Have I evaluated the success of that change?

Change is not something that most people embrace. It is typically born of necessity rather than by initiating proactive steps. But what do we gain by sitting back and waiting until we are forced to make change when there simply isn't a choice? We think that peace of mind results from staying within our comfort zones; it's a couch potato's nirvana. I've been there. But then some great mentors and advisors came along and shook up my frame of reference regarding what my life could mean and my practice could become. I sat up and took notice. I hope you'll do the same.

The transition and transformation from a basic financial planning practice to a life-planning model has changed my life, my practice and my relationship with my clients. On a personal level, I am now more focused, open and accessible to the possibilities of life, in the present and the future. It has opened the door to thinking a new way—more deeply and with greater meaning. My business has grown to five full-time advisors, two junior planners and three staff. Revenue, while affected by market conditions, is steady and growing. We see growth as natural and organic and are constantly looking to improve and add more members to our team. We operate in an organized, clear and concise manner, each of us benefiting by our individual and collective successes. Our clients are working toward living their dreams while dealing with life transitions and the unknowns that happen along the way. Financial Life Planning has affected everyone and everything we encounter, from how our office is arranged to our intention to live a balanced and happy life.

I invite you, as you read on, to look at your life, your business and your relationship with your clients in a new and open way, from the inside out. I invite you to pick up the gauntlet of change, knowing here and now that it is not easy, not a direct line and may not feel safe. Take comfort in the knowledge that it can be a wonderful experience, full of discovery, innovation, evolution and success. The destination might be unclear right now, but that's just fine. It's time to shake off the shackles of stultifying comfort and create a new beginning for you, your business and your clients. It is up to you, but you're not alone.

Part Three:
Inside

Chapter Four

Self-Inquiry: Where am I?

"The important thing is not to stop questioning."

~ Albert Einstein

I will assume that, as a successful business owner, you believe in investing. This chapter is intended to bring awareness. The process of gaining awareness requires time, concentration and effort. You might feel skeptical about spending precious time on this step. Please understand that this step is a profound and important investment.

We are self-created creatures of habit. This is certainly evident in how we work. Unless there is a halt to the pattern, we tend to keep doing what we always do. We approach our day in the same way; we follow a set of rituals and patterns that become normal for us. From the moment we wake up to the time we go to sleep, we follow patterns of behavior that provide us with a level of comfort. But do these patterns always serve us? I have a friend who reaches for his Blackberry every time he hears the "ding" of a new email. No matter what he's doing or interrupting, the ding sends him immediately to that little machine in the finest Pavlovian fashion.

Consider for a moment some of the things you do on a daily basis that are simply part of your routine, those simple things that have become mere habit. When you drive to work, do you always go the same route, even if there are several options? Do you put on your right shoe before your left? Do you brush your teeth using your dominant hand? What other rituals or habits have you created? Can you think of something in your professional life that you do just because you've always done it? It's not that these habits are wrong or right; it's merely a matter of one's awareness. See if the following scenario feels familiar:

There you are: puttin' in the hours, making calls, prospecting for new opportunities, meeting new clients, taking care of existing relationships. Are there too many items on your to-do list? The hours, days, weeks, months and yes, even years roll by with lightning speed. Wow. What the heck just happened?

We play a variety of roles in our lives as financial advisors. One moment we are the Financial Advisor, the next we are the Business Owner, and later, maybe, we are The Tired Person Who Is Finally Home From Work. Is it any wonder we sometimes get tied up in knots and forget the purpose behind what we do? There was a Broadway show in the early 1960s entitled "Stop the World, I Want to Get Off." How does that sound right about now? We devote hours of our lives working on matters whose true value we hardly consider. But we keep at it, because it's what we do. It is not that it's wrong, *but it might be.* Without taking the time to consider these questions, how do we truly know? We can easily find ourselves in a state of overwhelm. Like the hamster on the wheel, we just keep going, following a path that provides a set of outcomes. Have you stopped to consider whether those outcomes are the ones you want? Have you considered whether your end game is being met? Do you even have an end game?

Having met with clients over the last thirty years, I know that most people do not have defined goals or even the semblance of a game plan. Our job is to help them focus on their preferred futures and what I call their financial musts—those things they must do to feel financially satisfied. In order to effectively guide your clients to look inside to see what they might want to change on the outside, I believe you *must* first go through this process yourself. In so doing, you can understand how it feels to examine, focus, consider and decide on the various aspects of life. Isn't that what you ask your clients to do? Is it not your job to hold your clients' hands through this process while they look at aspects of their life that they've perhaps never before considered? Before you ask someone else to do that, it's time for you to do it yourself.

We all know what it's like to get so caught up in the "doing" that we forget the reason why we're doing in the first place. As I've described, for way too many years I would work from sun-up until late at night and then get up and do it all again, not knowing whether anything I'd done had value either on a short or long-term basis. My life was consumed by taking care of anything and everything that had to do with my business, regardless of the value to others or myself. I believed that if I just kept my head down and kept crossing items off the list, my clients would be happy and I would be successful. Money came in, money went out. Contacts or referrals somehow became clients. The files got stuffed with more folders, my day at the office got exponentially longer and more complicated. I was raised to believe that you just work and work and work, yet here I was—overweight and feeling trapped by the very machine I had built. As Walt Kelly said in his Pogo comic strip, "We have met the enemy and he is us!" So, what changed? What opened the gate of knowledge? I remembered my father.

My father, who passed away several years ago, was a schoolteacher and a musician—the consummate Depression era workaholic. When he wasn't teaching, correcting papers, writing lesson plans, tutoring, or working his second job as a club date musician, he was fixing, building, cleaning and taking care of the house. My dad was a rock—indestructible, strong, ceaselessly and seemingly effortlessly going from work to work to work to work. One night, when I was seven or eight, I heard him come home around 2:00 am from back-to-back club dates. I got up to say hello and found him sitting on a kitchen chair, motionless. He looked exhausted.

I went over to give him a hug and felt the wetness of his tuxedo, totally sweated through. This really shocked me. Every time I'd seen him on the bandstand, he was smiling and singing and seemed to be having so much fun. Now, though, he just didn't move. So I tugged at his sleeve and helped pull his jacket off, revealing the frilly white tuxedo shirt stuck to his body. After helping him remove his jacket, I undid his bowtie. He was still unable to move. I knelt down to untie his shoes, pulled them off and rubbed the underside of his feet, which were tender from standing for twelve hours next to his upright bass. I heard a tired sigh escape his lips, acknowledging the first pleasure of the day and the cumulative effect on his body of days, weeks, months and years of ceaseless doing. To this day, almost fifty years later, I can still recall his look of total exhaustion and pain. It is something that a youngster of seven or eight doesn't forget—a look of defeat, knowing that he would get up the next morning and do it all over again.

A few years later, I came home from school and found out that he had been admitted to the hospital for exhaustion. As was normal for that generation, this was referred to in hushed tones but never discussed. I was not surprised, just scared. Almost as scared as I was, fifty years later, when I saw the same look of exhaustion on my own face. I agreed to invest some time in self-inquiry. Immediately.

I spent the next day preparing, taking care of all the mandatory items on my to-do list for the next few days. For the first time in my adult life, I prepared myself to take a full day out of the office for a reason other than suffering from a contagious illness. I was excited to look at my future, but first needed to assess where I was in the present (other than overwhelmed).

Taking stock of your current reality is the first step in the inside-out process of considering where you are and whether there is a reason to consider changes. It can be a painful process if approached from a standpoint of self-criticism rather than the position of strength and adventure. What is vital is the willingness and ability to access your truth, lay it bare, and ask the important questions, which might indeed open the portal to new possibilities. This opening step is one of knowledge, not understanding. It is about putting the truth on the paper. No conclusions, no decisions. No judgments. Just write your truth. What you derive out of this assessment is directly related to your willingness to speak the truth.

The remainder of this chapter consists of a series of self-inquiry exercises. You might need several hours for each section. Find a place that is comfortable but without distractions. I suggest you find a place outside of the office where you can really focus; the phone and computer and staff are too tempting a distraction. Use whatever method of making notes works best for you and take your time. No one will see your answers but you. You will not be placed into neat little categories and you will not be provided with pat answers. The purpose of this self-assessment is to allow you the heady freedom to observe your starting point. It will help you use your assets to your best advantage.

Personal Assessment:

1. Draw a larger version of this circle on a separate page. Fill in the circle as a pie chart to represent the normal activities of your life by percentage. For example, consider work, personal time, family, vacation, education and so on.

2. Are you satisfied with your personal and family life? How would you rate or describe your family and personal life? Are important relationships being attended to, or are they taken for granted? Are there people who are important in your life who are not getting the attention you wish or are put on the 'back-burner' while you rationalize, "Oh, they'll understand"? How does this situation feel?

3. Are there aspects of your life about which you are especially passionate? List five things you are passionate about, and describe how much time you have devoted to them in the last sixty days. Scan the list, and select the one that captures your attention. Close your eyes and imagine yourself involved in that activity. What does it look like, in detail? What does it feel like? Is that feeling missing from your current life?

4. In what activities do you regularly participate, other than those that are work related?

5. How much time do you devote to your personal interests each week? Each month?

6. How many vacations have you taken within the last five years, where you spent more than five consecutive working days out of the office? I've talked about the need to "sharpen the saw," taking the time to refresh, regenerate and recover. Are you trying to cut down trees with a dull blade?

7. On your vacations, how many consecutive days away from the office did you typically take?

8. Do you routinely work more than fifty hours per week?

9. Let's look at how and where you spend your time. How much of your time is spent on "super critical" activities; how much is spent on important and necessary activities; how much is spent on activities that you probably shouldn't be doing or doing so much? Have you ever had the thought, Where did the months (or worse—years or decades) go?

10. Do you feel in control of all aspects of your personal, business and financial life? Is there an ease and flow to your life? Or is there pressure, causing feelings of panic or overwhelm? Can you accept that feeling in control is a gift you can give yourself?

11. Do you feel physically and mentally strong right now? Do you ever ask yourself how you're doing? How you're feeling physically and emotionally? Are there problems or issues that are being ignored or overlooked, simply because the answer would force you to do something? Are you getting exercise or living a basically sedentary lifestyle? Do you want to exercise more but keep putting it off because you're "too busy"?

12. How do you handle change? Can you recall a time when you've had to deal with a change or changes? Was it voluntary? What was it like? How did you do? What were the challenges? What did you learn?

13. What are your toughest personal challenges right now? See if you can write down a few challenges, big and small.

14. What kind of personal support system do you have? Who are those people in your life with whom you can totally be yourself, without fear or worry? Whom can you call when life feels overwhelming? Whom do you reach out to when you need an ear? Do you reach out?

Much can be learned from this assessment. You can see if you are living in balance personally—whether you are truly living a multidimensional life or are so single focused that most other areas are ignored or severely curtailed and likely to create significant problems in the future. Take a look at your pie chart. What can you infer from the breakdown of activities? Are there any bells going off in your mind? What areas need to be considered? Does anything concern you? If so, write some notes. Perhaps there are some items that might benefit from further consideration. When you feel ready, move on to the business assessment below.

Business Assessment:

1. What is your current business model? Does your current business format meet your needs for the present? Do you trade off convenience for appropriateness of structure? Do you have a partner? Is there an operating agreement and a buy-sell agreement? Are you aware of the liability you carry as part of that structure? Does this model support making changes?

2. Do you have a natural market or niche? Do you have a specialty? Where do your clients come from? Do you have a natural market or feeder system that regularly delivers your preferred clients to your door? Do you have connections with professionals or others who send great prospects to your door? If you do have these connections or markets, how do you ensure that they continue? What could threaten your ongoing success? When was the last time you introduced an innovation to your business? Everything changes, life changes, businesses change; have you? Your landscape may look safe and secure, but is it? How have the recent market downturns affected your business? What have you learned from this experience? What innovations could bring you greater long-term success?

3. What are your client demographics? If a significant portion of your clients are elderly and you don't know their heirs, what is the likelihood that you will have clients five or ten years into the future? Do your clients come from a particular industry? If so, what is happening in that industry, and how could that impact your business in the future? Are your strategies in alignment with the realities of your client base?

4. What is your client turnover? How many clients did you lose over the last several years? Were they valued relationships? Why did they leave? Was it your choice or theirs? What went wrong? What might you have done to maintain those relationships? Could you have done something different or better to keep them with your firm? Where did they come from originally? Could those losses create problems with the referral sources? What lessons have been learned? What did you do with what you learned?

5. Where do your new clients come from? Has this process changed since you began your business? Do you know how every client wound up at your door? If not, why not? Do you see the value of this information?

6. What changes have occurred in your business in the last five years? Has your business grown? If so, how? If not, why not? Can you look back over the five-year span and assess those changes? Have they been positive? Quantify the results.

7. What changes have occurred in your industry in the last five years? Which trends have emerged, and which trends have faded away? How have they affected your practice? Are they likely to? Why? Or Why not? Can you see the value of this knowledge?

8. What are the biggest challenges you confront today? Hiring and retaining employees? Growing your business? Technology? Unrealistic demands of clients? Not enough time in your day? Not enough revenue? List them all. Start with the really BIG ones.

9. What changes have occurred in society or globally that impact your business? How have these changes affected your business?

10. What are your revenue sources? Are they repeating and regular? What is the nature of your earnings? Are they commission based? Do you require a fresh batch of clients each year to replace that commission action, or do you need to continue to create transactions in order to create revenue? What percentage of your revenue is from recurring fees, rather than transactional? How has this situation changed over the last several years? What are your trends? If you are commission reliant, have you seen a decrease in rates? Which pressures exist, and which pressures do you anticipate in the (near and long-term) future?

11. Do you have an exit strategy? What is the perfect scenario for your exit? What is your end game? How have you prepared for the time you wish to leave? What if you want to leave but can't, or want to stay on but can't? Are you prepared?

12. What would happen to your business if you became incapacitated or dropped dead? What would happen to your clients? Your family? Who would service your clients? How would your family receive value for your practice? What liability would transfer to your family if something happened? What would happen to your employees?

Review your answers. There might be areas, such as client demographics, which you might need to research to answer fully. Yes, I know you have tons of things to do, but trust me. This is where your investment on your business today will pay big profits in the future.

When you're ready, move on to the final assessment. I would guess that by this time, there's a good deal of information and thought going on inside your brain. I want to remind you that this process is not about judgment; it's about careful observation. As you prepare for this last section of the self-assessment, you might want to take a walk and clear your head to allow yourself to proceed with focus.

Financial Assessment:

1. How much income do you earn? How much gross revenue have you earned on an annual basis over the last five years? Do you understand your numbers and take ownership of them?

2. What are your net earnings (profits) over the last five years? How much did you get to keep for all your efforts? Is it enough?

3. Is there a trend evident in these numbers? Is your business on an up curve, a down curve or a flat line? What, if anything, can be inferred from the numbers over the last five years?

4. How much salary/earnings have you extracted out of the business over the last five years? What's left after the expenses of running your business? Are you earning a living commensurate with your ability and the time you put in? What are you earning on an hourly basis? What do you get paid to do?

5. Do you carry ongoing balances on your credit cards? Are you in debt? How long have you been carrying debt? How much do you owe? Is consumer debt part of your ongoing lifestyle? When was the last time you had zero balances on your cards and were debt free?

6. Is your cash flow predictable? Can you track with any reasonable level of expectation how much income you will earn, when it will be received and from which sources? Can you reasonably predict your annual income?

7. Has your net worth grown each of the last five years? Can you chart the increase in your net worth over the last five years? Can you objectively review the growth in your assets or the decrease in debt?

8. Do you feel money pressures? Do you have ease with money? Does money represent conflict or pressure in your life? If so, make some notes as to your feelings, opinions, observations and thoughts.

9. Do you know your credit score? If so, what is it? Is it where it needs to be? If not, why not? What will it take to move it in the right direction?

10. Are your taxes filed and paid on a timely basis? Do you file your taxes without interest and penalties?

11. How much time do you spend on your personal finances? Do you have a financial plan? Do you devote adequate and appropriate time to your own personal finances? Is your house in order?

12. Do you work with a CPA who prepares your taxes and serves as your financial advisor? Do you value professional advice?

13. Do you have a current Will, trust and/or estate protection documents? Are they updated to include all pertinent changes and life events?

14. Is your personal recordkeeping system effective? Come on, put it on the line; do you have a system? Does it work?

15. How well are you aware of your expenses? Fixed? Discretionary? Savings? Investments?

Congratulations! You have completed a very important step! You have thought about and observed your current status in terms of your personal, business and financial life. What did you learn? What became evident? How did it feel? I suggest you gather and organize your notes and set up three new pages. On the top of the first page write: "Super Critical;" on the second page write: "Important and Necessary", and on the third page: "It Would be Great, But …" Then on each page, make three columns titled "Personal," "Business" and "Financial." Select one, or at most two, items from your notes that fit each category as "Super Critical," "Important and Necessary" and "It Would be Great, But …" Then, write down what you've learned from all the steps in this process.

Your assessment is your jumping-off point for looking inside at what remains viable and valued. Once this is clear, you can more easily decide and implement changes on the outside to better create the life of your dreams. Your work in this chapter will be your blueprint for change and the critical reference point for the rest of our work together. When you're ready for the next step, turn the page.

Chapter Five

Exploring: Looking In and Looking Out

"Twenty years from now you will be more disappointed by the things you didn't do than by the ones you did do. So throw off the bowlines. Sail away from the safe harbor. Catch the trade winds in your sails. Explore. Dream. Discover."

~ Mark Twain

You've answered a whole bunch of probing questions. You've hopefully amassed some useful data about yourself and your current situation. Now is the time to examine what you've discovered and to synthesize all that data into a cogent and meaningful arrangement. This process is essential to clarifying what exactly will bring you greater satisfaction personally and professionally.

As financial planners, we are called upon to absorb tons of data and put it into context. Looking at the technical information and melding it with our clients' hopes and dreams is a course of action that includes internal and external forces. I call this process "Looking in and looking out." You will learn about your own areas of challenge, as well as be better able to understand and empathize with your clients as they go through this process themselves.

Looking in and looking out is a way of taking in information and viewing it both from a distance and up close. You will be activating both sides of your brain. The act of looking in and looking out means consciously, intentionally, asking yourself: What do I *think* about that issue? How do I *feel* about it? Accessing both hemispheres of your brain can be a workout because most of us are more comfortable with one side rather than the other. Just like learning any new activity, it will take some practice. So, for those "Quants" who might be feeling a little queasy at the thought of having to explore the "touchy-feely" side, and for those "Quals" out there who run away from numbers, facts, charts, reports and other sources of factual detail, I say, take a nice deep breath. This won't hurt a bit ... well, hardly at all.

In the last chapter, you assessed various aspects of your life. Read through your notes several times, and see if your answers are complete. Does your self-assessment ring true? Is it honest? Have you avoided any tough issues? If any alterations, additions or new thoughts have occurred to you, feel free to make those corrections. If not, great. Let's go eat the elephant!

As Financial Life Planners, we can help clients reduce the size and scope of large life issues into more manageable pieces. This is equally true for us in our personal lives and our roles as business owners. You are wrestling with big stuff, so the next step is to break down the issues you came across in your assessment. Your objective is to explore your thoughts and feelings regarding the areas of least comfort. If you bump up against something uncomfortable, don't run away from it. Mentally note it, be willing to acknowledge the fact that there is discomfort, record it and move on. I suggest that as you record your responses to the questions below, codify your statements with "C" or "D" for *comfort* or *discomfort*. I've learned a lot from going back to my old notes and noticing what I felt comfortable and uncomfortable with. The change is only too obvious.

I emphasize the importance of writing down your thoughts and feelings because this process brings clarity and definition to your thoughts. When something is just in your head, it doesn't have the same form or substance as putting it in writing. The step of writing your answers down takes your realizations from the intangible to the tangible.

Personal Assessment:

1. What have you learned from answering the questions on personal assessment? (Make a list of factual statements. "I have learned …")

2. What is working well for you? What is worth celebrating and appreciating?

3. What could be done differently or better? (Again, make a list, and make it factual. You may wish to use bullet points. For example, "I could take more time off.")

4. What is your level of personal satisfaction? (Perhaps use a scale of 1-10, with 10 being the highest.)

5. What are your *thoughts* about your answers? (Left brain—make it factual.)

6. How do you *feel* about your answers? (Right brain—rely on your emotions: happy, sad, anxious, elated, depressed, worried.)

Business Assessment:

1. What have you learned from your responses to the business assessment? (Again, make a list.)

2. What is working well? What is worth celebrating and appreciating?

3. What could be done differently or better? (Again, make a list, and make it factual. For example, "I could create a better process for …")

4. What is your level of satisfaction in regard to your business, from 1-10?

5. What do you *think* about your business assessment? (Left brain—make it factual.)

6. How do you *feel* about this assessment? (Right brain—rely on your emotions: happy, sad, anxious, elated, depressed, worried.)

Financial Assessment:

1. What have you learned from your financial assessment?

2. What are you most proud of?

3. What causes you concern, if anything?

4. Rate your level of satisfaction, again from 1-10.

5. What do you *think* about your financial assessment? (Left brain—make it factual.)

6. What are your *feelings* on this topic? (Right brain—rely on your emotions: happy, sad, anxious, elated, depressed, worried.)

Finished? No, not quite. Go back to all your points and look at the "Cs" and "Ds." Where are you comfortable? Compile all your "Cs," and transcribe your comforts into a list beginning with the most comfortable to the least. Do the same for your "Ds," listing the greatest discomforts to the least. This will become your priority list for future reference. The information derived here is the basis for your next step.

Chapter Six

Deciding: Folding or Going All In

"You don't drown by falling in the water;
you drown by staying there."

~ Edwin Louis Cole

All of your work thus far has been an effort to look inside yourself and your practice in order to gather information for your next steps towards building a life of balance, a purposeful existence and a business that better helps you, your team and your clients through the journey of life. Financial Life Planning facilitates that journey, because it asks the questions pertinent to creating and living a life that is authentic and meaningful to you.

This chapter will assist you in deciding whether to fold your cards or to go all in. There is no middle path. Once you decide to make a change, whether huge or tiny, it's time to give it your all. Will you decide to do nothing or something? What will you decide to do now, and what will you focus on later? You have the power to assess, gauge what's important, and decide; no one can do this for you. Right now, you are standing on the edge of a decision. While you might recognize that some adjustments are necessary, you might find that there are obstacles. For example, you may feel resistant, because you just can't see what your life will look like once you've made these changes. The next chapter will deal with this issue. For now, we'll sharpen the focus by analyzing the positive aspects of change and aligning them against what might possibly be the downsides of change.

Go back through your notes from the last two chapters. For each item that would involve making a change, write down both the potential pros and cons of making this change. Examine your list again. What rings true for you? Have you found a direction or a sense of priority? Make a list of changes you want to make, separated in the three categories of personal, business and finance.

Another aspect of "deciding" is engaging in conversation with others whom you respect and work with. Who are the stakeholders? They might include employees, family, a mentor, friends, business colleagues, or professionals, such as your CPA or attorney. For example, after I made the decision to make changes in my practice, I wanted to hear other points of view. I shared my thoughts with my assistant and asked for questions or comments. I had similar conversations with my accountant, family members, my mentor and my best friend. The purpose of these conversations was to gather questions rather than to collect answers. It was a rich and rewarding experience, because the people I spoke with became excited about the prospect of these changes. Some of the comments were cautionary and provided good fuel for further consideration. For example, my CPA expressed concern that there were not many advisors doing what I was attempting and therefore, there wasn't a body of work to rely on to help avoid pitfalls or problems. As a result, I sought out several advisors who had already made the leap and found that while there were obstacles, they hadn't experienced anything I didn't think I could overcome.

One note of caution: At this stage in the process, you may have less confidence in your potential choices. For this reason, you are more susceptible to bias and pressure from others to alter your decision. *Choose the right people to talk to.* Be clear that you are asking for comments and questions because you value their input, but the decision is ultimately yours. Be aware that most, if not all, people are hard-wired to resist change. Seek out those who have experienced significant change in their own lives or careers. You may also need to prepare yourself to listen to others' reactions. Are you open and ready to hear? Are you bringing negative thoughts into the discussion? Listen carefully to your internal conversations regarding people's negative reactions. Ask yourself if their reasoning and reactions are sound or simply knee-jerk. After your conversations, note how your attitude towards the pros and cons may have shifted. At this point, you should be very clear about what you will decide to change.

Deciding is the last step in the contemplation process. From here we move ahead to preparation. Your past has been fully examined. It's time to look ahead!

Chapter Seven

Visioning: Beginning at the End

"Vision without action is a daydream. Action without vision is a nightmare."

~ Japanese Proverb

Congratulations. You've courageously made the decision to make changes in your life and practice. Big stuff! Now what? Now that you are consciously and intentionally moving in a new direction, we want to continue with momentum and strength. It's time to make it real.

You've devoted great care and energy in the stages of Self-Inquiry, Exploring and Deciding; the next step is Visioning. As Stephen Covey stated in his seminal work, *The Seven Habits of Highly Effective People,* "Begin with the end in mind."[11] The step of visioning allows one to create an internal picture of the future.

Let's say you want to drive from New York to California. You wouldn't normally just jump in the car and drive. There are a few things to consider. Is the car fit for the trip? Is there gas in the car? Which routes do I take? What costs will I encounter? How much money will I need? Am I physically and mentally prepared for the long drive? What will I need to bring with me? How long will the trip take? What will I do when I get there? Where is "there"? What will the weather be like on my trip? Is that a consideration? Do I need a GPS? Are my maps accurate? You may notice that each question leads into another; as you write your vision, the same process occurs.

There are two steps to visioning. The first is the internal process of imagining, and the second is capturing your thoughts in writing, separating what you know from what you need to know and creating workable action steps. In past exercises, I asked you to access both the thinking and feeling aspects of your brain. Do so again here. As you create your vision, you will find that some of your visioning is very creative, while other segments are pure nuts and bolts.

For some people, the word "visioning" conjures up images like a crystal ball or a melodramatic seer dressed in flowing robes. I am asking you to do something far more practical. In this case, I am not asking you to go into a trance, light incense or ingest any funny substances (unless, of course, this helps you with your process.) I just want you to give yourself the gift of time, space, focus, and especially *intentional imagination*. This is not a process to rush through. Give yourself adequate time to allow your thoughts and ideas to marinate and coalesce. The essential element of imagination is necessary to bring the pieces together. When you were a child, this was a natural process. You could be anyone, anywhere, at any time. I remember spending a lot of time of my childhood being Mickey Mantle. I could see the vivid green of the Yankee Stadium turf, smell the hot dogs and hear the vendors screaming, "Beer here!" over the roar of the crowd. I could even imitate his limp as he brought his taped-up body around the bases after another mammoth home run. My power, talent and accomplishments were limitless!

Does this sound like dreaming? Like fantasy? No problem. Beginning with your ideal is the strongest place to start. Think big! Have you ever heard the acronym BHAG? I've heard it over the years at seminars for advisors who want to grow their businesses; it stands for *Big Hairy Audacious Goal*. This is the time to picture your ideal future in all its glory. Make it huge; make it amazing; make it *yours!*

Time to get started. Find a space away from as many distractions as possible. In order to be effective, focus is critical. There are many books written on visioning exercises, such as *Visioning: Ten Steps to Designing the Life of Your Dreams,* by Lucia Capacchione. Here is one method:[12]

Close your eyes. Take several deep breaths and keep your mind focused on the air coming in and out of your nostrils. Try to keep your mind as quiet as possible. Once you feel relaxed, ask yourself these questions:

What would _____ look like if it were perfect? (For example: What would my office set-up look like if it were perfect?)

What aspect of _____ would be critical? (For example: What aspect of my office set-up would be critical?)

Who would do it? (For example: Who would be responsible for setting up the office?)

How would it be done? (For example: How would the new office be set up? What are the specific steps?)

Another method of visioning involves putting yourself into the ideal picture—literally. Imagine yourself already there. How would it feel, look, seem? What would the reactions be from others? Why? After asking the questions above for our new office set-up, I went on to create the following vision. In addition to the questions above, I asked myself: What experience do I want our clients to enjoy? What does our space look like? How does it flow? How can we ensure that the space promotes the feelings we wish to engender? Who has the knowledge to help us do this? Here is an example of my vision for our new office environment at Financial Focus, LLC.

When a client walks into our offices, they are first greeted by the sight of fresh flowers on the reception desk. The air in the office feels and smells fresh and is a comfortable temperature. The walls are painted a bright happy color, the lighting is bright without being harsh and there is pleasing and inspiring artwork on the walls. There is a fish tank with lively colorful fish. The area is orderly, clean and organized. The magazines are current: news, design, lifestyle and other areas of interest. There are no copies of the Wall Street Journal *or other financial publications. Soft music is playing to help make the atmosphere relaxing.*

Our receptionist greets our clients cheerfully by name, inviting them to have a seat on the couch or chairs. She introduces herself if they have never been in before and offers to take their coats and put them in our closet. She asks if they would care for a beverage and promptly fills that request. In the case of existing relationships, she already knows their preferences and reaffirms if they still wish for that today. Meanwhile, she notifies the advisor that the client is present. When instructed, she ushers the clients into the conference room. In the conference room, the clients find water by their places, along with a pad of paper, a pen, and a copy of our meeting agenda. On the conference table is a bowl of chocolates and a box of tissues; at the head of the table is a folder, pad, calculator and pen. There is a laptop on the sideboard. There is a clean white board next to the head of the table. The walls are lined with bookcases filled with books that cover a multitude of topics dealing with all aspects of planning. The artwork on the walls is interesting and appealing. The room is clean, professional and comfortable, giving the appearance of organization and, most of all, great attention to detail.

The client experience is duplicated each time someone walks into our office. Because of this reinforcement, our clients cannot help but see us as professional, consistent and caring. They feel comfortable and respected. They find that they enjoy coming here.

There is great energy and joy in creating a vision. Remember, the greater the level of detail, the more real and attainable it becomes. As you move through the exercise, let yourself feel the excitement that builds around the vision of reaching your goal and seeing your idea become a reality. Try not to get bogged down by irrelevant issues or doubts about practicality; you can deal with that later. Go into great detail. Enjoy yourself!

After you have your vision clearly in mind, translate it into writing. Take the mind pictures and turn them into words or drawings. I am a huge fan of mind-mapping, a technique that helps me lay out my thoughts in a non-linear but organized fashion. Getting all that information out of your head and onto paper or your computer screen is essential in taking your vision from thought to action. Again, spare no detail. New ideas will undoubtedly emerge as you put your vision into words. If questions arise, write them down on a separate piece of paper that you can come back to later. Keep the vision pure and filled with assurance and joy.

At a recent staff meeting, I challenged my colleagues to create a vision of their life five years in the future. My purpose was two-fold; one was to assess the vision of each team member to get an idea of their thinking, and the second was to help them motivate and inspire themselves to achieve the dream they described. The following is one example of this exercise. After I read this vision for the first time, I asked my colleague what impact this visioning exercise had, if any. His response was remarkable. He told me that after writing it, he felt energized, focused and even more excited about being a part of our Financial Focus family. I hope you enjoy reading this as much as I have.

> It is a Saturday afternoon in July of 2013. I am forty-five years old—and in better shape than I was at thirty-five. Nancy is forty-four, still thriving in her career, and almost never working at night anymore. Emma is almost ten and starting in the third grade in the fall. Christopher has just turned six and will start kindergarten in two months. My mom and dad are still around, and so are my mother-in-law and her boyfriend.
>
> I am hosting a Financial Focus "employee appreciation event." This is a barbecue at our new house. (I can't stand sawdust, so I don't think we'll be expanding the current house.) Financial Focus is now twenty-two people!!! And we invited their families, so there's like eighty people at this thing!
>
> Financial Focus is now ten senior advisors, a COO, a compliance person, two para-planners, three junior advisors, four staff and Anna! Even though it wasn't an objective, the five new senior advisors are as diverse as the first five. Ethnically and otherwise. This is an eclectic group, my friend! And we are rocking.

Our office is actually not an office, but a huge two-story house. Each floor has six offices with windows on the outside, surrounding a bullpen of six cubes on the inside. There's one big and one small conference rooms on each floor. The first floor has an awesome reception area. The coolest thing about this place is the sports room on the second floor. Big flat screen TV, wet bar, comfortable couches and a pool table. Canadiens game, anyone?

Now, for the numbers. I am handling fifty families, with $50M under management, and ongoing Financial Life Plans for all of them. I am now making $300k per year, while working 176 days. (That's four days a week for forty-four weeks; eight weeks off, no Fridays!)

I spend almost all of my time meeting with clients or prospects. Meeting with clients means the annual renewal meetings, the presentation or monitoring of the Financial Life Plan, or just relationship-building meetings. All of the tactical investment-related activities are handled by one of the junior advisors (rebalancing, trades, wires, allocation, etc.). All the meeting materials are also produced by the junior advisor. All of the data gathering for the plans is also done by the junior advisor and the para-planner. I basically come up with the scenarios and the planning memo outline.

I also spend a lot of time in interaction with the other members of the firm. With the senior advisors, that means meeting regularly to discuss particular client cases so we can all learn from each other. Experience cannot be bought, but that's as close as it gets. It also means spending a lot of time with the junior advisors as a mentor. I benefited from the veterans' time when I was a junior, and I feel it's important to give back. Plus, one of those might succeed me down the road ...

Michael has started introducing another senior advisor to every single one of his relationships. He is not ready to be put out to pasture just yet, but we're smartly handling his slowing down in terms of hours. One of the other eight senior advisors is Michael's successor as the visionary of Financial Focus. Not clear in my head who that is yet ...

The ownership of Financial Focus is now held by more than one person, and I am one of them. And I will eventually have a successor of my partial ownership. This thing will transcend us all.

The COO is one of the key persons in the business. He/she can concentrate on running the business side of things (including all processes and human resources) so we can concentrate on being Financial Life Planners. Maybe the COO is the same person as the visionary. Maybe the COO is a part owner, too.

So what am I doing with my 189 free days a year? I am now coaching Christopher's hockey team ... which I plan to do for the next twelve years! Anybody involved in hockey in New Jersey knows that means very early mornings and faraway places. In other words, a big time commitment. But again, I have thousands of hours to give back to very many people in that particular area.

I'm also teaching in a CFP program. If you think our profession is hot now, just you wait! It will be huge in five years, and I'll be there to push it forward. Maybe involved in the FPA nationally, but that's probably another five years out.

And every four years I attend the Winter Olympics with the whole family. We went for the first time to Vancouver in 2010. That was an experience of a lifetime, so we'll never miss another one.

And by the way, the office barbecue in 2018 will also be at our house ... our new shore house somewhere in New Jersey. God knows how many people will be at THAT thing ..."

This vision brings a smile to my face every time I read it—a smile that says, *What a great dream,* not a smirk that says, *Yeah, right!* Notice how his vision describes his personal life balance, his satisfaction with work, and what he would like to see happen, right down to the "big flat screen TV, wet bar, comfortable couches and pool table." He knows how much he wants to work and play as well as what is happening with his family and the manifestation of his values. The who, what, where, when and what! Get the picture?

The next part of visioning is called the "brain dump." The key to the brain dump is to identify what you know and what you don't know and to render the overall vision into manageable pieces. Building your vision from the ground up is critical. In other words, start with the grand dream, break it down to the basics and then progress until you have achieved the level of detail that enables you to create action steps. It is the act of breaking down the vision into small and achievable pieces. For example, when converting my vision of our office environment into reality, I created a mind-map that was broken down into categories such as Personnel, Reception Area, Conference Room, Tools and Technology, and Miscellaneous. Under the "Reception Area" category, I listed the all the details of what would go into creating that space as per my vision (the look, feel, smell). Under "Personnel," I needed to understand who was involved in the process, what that person was responsible for, and how I wanted it accomplished (for example, checking the data base before the meeting to check drink preferences). Under the "Tools and Technology," I listed the needs for the space (aromatherapy diffuser, music player, white board, markers, computer, calculator, etc.). The more you make it real, the easier it is to translate your thoughts into writing and then into action.

Next, prioritize these small steps. What needs to come first, and what can wait? Once you've established your priorities, look at what you know and what you don't know. For those items where you don't have sufficient information, knowledge or experience, you'll need to find out where to get that data. That is a critical next step. You can put what you know on the back burner in favor of what you don't, since the unknown information can change your thinking when facts are uncovered or realized. For example, when I first created my first draft and began to break down the steps, I found that it would have been too costly to hire someone initially to fill one of the roles I had considered. I had to realign my thoughts with my economic reality, knowing that eventually, I would fill that role when the funds were available.

Let's take the next step with your list of unknowns. It's time to uncork your network. In other words, start asking questions! For example, in putting together our office space, I needed to consult with someone who understood about lighting, office flow, storage space, technology, wiring, office setup, furniture requirements and decor. I spoke with a Feng Shui consultant to help with the concepts of walls, doors, color, decor and other items. I met with our technology specialist and explained my vision and what was necessary to accomplish that goal. I worked with an architect and furniture specialist to help design the office space and workflow. I asked lots of questions and sought input from those who had the knowledge and experience I lacked.

Go to your colleagues, peers, professional associations and professionals in other fields and ask if they have access to this information or if not, who do they know who might. You might use your local university's business department as a resource. The Internet contains a wealth of information that can fill in the blanks. The key is to make your questions concise and specific. If your questions are too vague, the chances of receiving specific answers are greatly diminished.

As you gather missing information, fill in the blanks and keep your focus on the open items. Your goal here is to gain knowledge, understanding and sufficient data to move forward with confidence. As you gather data, you most likely will find that more questions arise. One answer might prompt an array of questions. Don't panic: this is normal. We learn the most from what we don't know, just as we learn much more from our "failures" than from our successes.

Be aware that at times, while in the middle of all the data, you might feel removed from your vision. For example, in building the office space, I remember feeling so bogged down by the details of colors, carpet, window treatments, wiring, computer needs, phone systems, modular units and work flow issues that I began to lose sight of my overall goals. So I went back to my vision statement and reread my vision daily of how, why, where, when it all fits together. I found that by doing so, I was able to keep that vision strong, real and purposeful. When I was overwhelmed by the banality of choosing carpet colors, reading my vision helped me keep a grasp of how it all fit together. I reminded myself to imagine how I would feel when I achieved those goals; how my life and business would change once I was able to accomplish my dreams.

Remember, the vision and dream is uniquely yours. It is the cornerstone of what is to come, the underpinning and rationale behind your actions. Your vision may change; in fact, it most probably will. When it does, you will make the appropriate corrections to get you aligned with your new destination, which is getting closer and closer. You are now ready to move into the next phase of change and begin manifesting your new reality.

Chapter Eight

Positioning: The Transition from Thought to Action

"One important key to success is self-confidence. An important key to self-confidence is preparation."

~ Arthur Ashe

My hope is that right now your brain is crackling and sizzling with the vivid vision of your life, your practice and your dreams. You've gone through all the thought exercises; you've assessed, decided and created your vision. Now it's time to move from thought to action. This next step is called Positioning because it puts you in the *position* to actually change your life, your business and your relationships with clients.

There are three main categories of positioning: positioning yourself, your business and your clients. The order in which we will discuss these points, and the order in which you approach them, is important. I believe that one needs to work internally first, making whatever personal modifications or changes are necessary. This prepares you to work on your business and then ultimately with, and for, your clients. Therefore, we will begin with a discussion of personal needs in positioning, then discuss aspects of your business that require review and perhaps alterations. Finally, we'll focus on positioning with clients, both existing and new, for the purpose of introducing them to your new business model.

Positioning Yourself:

As Arthur Ashe said, it takes confidence and preparation to experience success. Preparation includes the acquisition of necessary competencies, which in turn increase your confidence. What are the competencies that you must acquire? Dick Zalack, entrepreneur, coach and founder of Focus Four®, called the essential competencies KASH: Knowledge, Attitude, Skills and Habits.[13] Does your current level of KASH match the requirements of your new practice? In most cases your level of KASH may be appropriate for what you are doing, but as you grow and change there will be gaps between where you are and where you want to be. It's important to know what you know, and even more important to know what you *don't* know. Therefore, an assessment and learning process is required.

The idea of KASH can be applied to all areas of one's life. For example, let's say you wish to learn to play tennis. Perhaps in your younger days, you batted the ball around the court with reckless, sweaty abandon. Here you are, a few years older, having put the racquet in the closet for all these years. What will it take to be a decent player today? What knowledge, attitude, skills and habits must you adopt?

- Take tennis lessons. (Knowledge)

- Remain open to learning new skills. (Attitude)

- Practice what you learn during lessons, such as becoming proficient at serving consistently. (Skills)

- Begin and end with lots of stretching. (Habits)

The same is true for shifting into your new model. What Knowledge, Attitudes, Skills or Habits do you need to change or acquire in order to be positioned to offer Financial Life Planning to your clients? What personal habits, skills and knowledge do you need to make your vision a reality? Is your attitude appropriate to fulfill your vision? Let's look at these KASH categories and how they relate to the changes you want to make in your personal life, your business and your work as a financial advisor.

Knowledge:

Acquiring knowledge provides the first level in building confidence. How do you feel when you *know* you know something? You feel powerful and capable! That's exactly where I want you to be. I recall the many questions that swirled through my mind as I was in the positioning process. What don't I know? What attitude will help me get where I need to go? How do I get there? Where do I get this information?

As part of my own positioning process, I realized that I needed to understand the principles and tools of Financial Life Planning and how to apply them consistently and meaningfully. I needed to learn how to integrate Life Planning with traditional Financial Planning to turn the process into a synergistic whole. I wanted to learn about the community of Life Planners and what they were doing; I needed to find the knowledge sources. Who created Financial Life Planning? Who is teaching it? Who has a platform most appropriate for my style and my needs? While unearthing these missing chunks of knowledge, I realized that I also needed to be familiar with the abundance of resources out there, such as books and workshops. Ultimately, I would need to experience these tools first hand in order to get a taste of what my clients would be experiencing.

To obtain this knowledge, I had to be willing to invest the time and financial resources necessary to experience Life Planning and be educated about how to practice it. I spoke with other advisors and listened to what they were doing. I soon discovered many pathways to the same goal; the key was to pinpoint the methodologies that resonated most deeply with my spirit and mind. After a great deal of research, I selected Money Quotient®, a non-profit organization responsible for many effective tools used by successful Life Planners. My research culminated with attending the three-day Money Quotient training, which gave me a full experience of the life-changing power of this methodology.

In addition to taking the M.Q. Fundamentals of Financial Life Planning training, I attended George Kinder's two-Day Seven Stages of Money

Maturity® workshop. The experience was incredibly rich and meaningful for me on a personal level and gave me additional insight into the power of Financial Life Planning.

As I hoped, these training sessions opened my mind to the myriad thoughts, feelings and opportunities that can result from participating in Life Planning exercises. Furthermore, my participation in these workshops enhanced my sensitivity and receptivity towards those who are apprehensive about delving into their money and life issues. I learned a great deal during my journey through this phase. One fact that remains clear is that gaining knowledge doesn't end; there's always more, and that is wonderful!

You may want to pause at this point and make a list of the knowledge you want to gain and how you could go about acquiring it.

Attitude:

Attitude is all about your mental approach. Your attitude directly influences how you see your personal and professional self, and how you view and relate to your clients, colleagues, employees and business. Breaking it down a bit further, attitude consists of four basic elements: integrity, clarity, consistency and a positive mental approach.

As a life planner, your own integrity is vital to your personal, business and clients' success. This commitment is so important that in our firm, our attitude about Financial Life Planning is, "It's not what we do, it's who we are." Life Planning initiates with who you are and expands into every aspect of your life and business. For example, one of the fundamental goals of Financial Life Planning is living a life of balance. Therefore, in order to have integrity as a planner, you must be actively pursuing your own goals of life balance. How would you advise a client to find life balance if you are working eighty hour weeks, out of shape and a personal mess? It's important that, as a planner, you are not saying one thing and doing another.

Like integrity, clarity means knowing beyond a doubt that you are moving along your path with purpose. There's an end in mind. It's not fuzzy, it's defined: you know what you're doing and why you're doing it. Clarity regarding your goals, vision, and purpose assists you in staying focused on these goals and therefore able to make good decisions. Clarity is like walking into a dark room and turning on the lights; it minimizes the chance of tripping over the furniture!

Consistency is another aspect of attitude that supports your integrity and success. When you decide to be a Financial Life Planner, it cannot be part time. In order to be successful, you and your staff must be consistent. This means that everyone understands what is expected, what their roles are, and how they fit into the bigger picture. This consistency assures that your clients will have positive interactions with everyone on your team. It allows clients to feel at ease as you are building your relationship. Bottom line: in order to generate consistency with your staff and clients, you must display it yourself.

Personally I found this to be a surprising challenge, even with the full understanding of its positive impact. When I looked at my own behavior, I found that the one thing I had a hard time doing consistently was staying organized and focused. Each day began with the mini crisis of facing my desk and the chaotic mess that invariably covered it. I was great at being consistently disorganized; I needed to make a shift in the other direction. Every evening before leaving the office, I began clearing off my desk. I put a sticky note on my computer screen, reminding me to clean the desk at the end of each day. After two weeks, the note was unnecessary as I greatly enjoyed the clarity that came with a well-organized space first thing in the morning. This small shift, done consistently, made a great difference in my productivity and attitude.

The last aspect of attitude concerns having a positive mental approach. Let's face it, without this, the rest falls apart under its own weight. When you maintain a positive mental approach, you are better able to bring the best of yourself everyday with energy and enthusiasm. You are able to concretize your ability to improve your own life and the lives of your co-workers and clients. A great positive mental attitude is like fuel. It's also infectious, motivating not only you but also clients and staff. This attitude helps your colleagues and staff feel important, that they have purpose and are part of something great. It keeps the bar high with expectation for continued success. So much can be accomplished by maintaining this great attitude; tasks seem easier and obstacles less daunting. You can recognize the success around you and show gratitude in a meaningful and open way, resulting in increased confidence within yourself and in those around you. How could one possibly succeed without it?

Like everyone else, in order to become an effective advisor, I too needed to examine my own life to see where I could improve my attitude. There couldn't be any disconnect between what I teach and how I live. I scrutinized the areas of my life—financial, personal, health, spirituality, community, and so on—to make sure I was living according to my values and integrity. I was happy to see that in most areas I was right on track. There was, however, one glaring exception. What screamed at me was the fact that I was totally out of shape and overweight from a lifetime of sedentary living, lack of exercise, too much work, and lack of balance and self-respect. This had to stop!

My first step was to envision a healthy, active, balanced life. Then I researched the many resources out there and created a plan that most resonated for me. It wasn't always easy to stick to, but I had made my decision. Remaining overweight and out of shape was not an option. I found the support I needed but most of all, my attitude was the glue that kept it all together. The results were a total change in my life, which resulted in losing over eighty pounds. While not perfect, my health and body are vastly improved, my stamina and energy are supercharged and my self-vision is reborn. Exercise and healthy eating are now habits that create more balance in my life. Even though these changes were very personal, my staff, partners and clients have all benefited from the increase in energy and self-confidence brought about by my ongoing health regime. It wasn't easy, but it's definitely worth it. Let's face it—we are all works in progress. Right attitude is the fuel that will support your efforts every step of the way.

Skills:

Financial Life Planning requires a variety of skill sets that might seem obvious but still warrant discussion. A few of the skills especially helpful in the positioning process are:

1. Being an empathetic and engaged listener

2. Helping clients work with, and through, the appropriate exercises and tools

3. Helping clients overcome obstacles by offering options and providing advice or referrals to those in a better position to help

4. Seeing the big picture and absorbing the details while remaining focused on the essential issues

    a. One needs to be able to ferret out the items that are not essential and focus on those that will aid the client in attaining their goals and dreams.

    b. Being a good planner means to be able to understand the numbers and the impact of what they mean, framed by the client's unique goals.

5. Remaining objective and non-judgmental

6. Communicating effectively

    a. Saying it like it is, not necessarily how the client would like to see it

    b. Knowing when and how to announce the elephant in the room

    c. Knowing what is needed at the right time: sometimes, it is silence; sometimes it is not

7. Delegating

    a. Knowing the outcome you desire, deciding who is best to handle the function, and that ensuring it gets done

8. Managing time effectively

We will discuss many of these items in future chapters. For now, ask yourself which of these or other skills you would benefit from enhancing.

Habits:

A tourist walks up to a guy on the streets of New York City and asks, "How do I get to Carnegie Hall?" Without batting an eye, the New Yorker says, "Practice!"

Well folks, that's what building a skill is all about: practice with the intent of creating great habits. We all have habits—some good, some perhaps a little frayed around the edges—but we all have them, from brushing our teeth in the morning to our bedtime rituals. The goal is to take the knowledge, skills and attitudes we've been talking about and turn them into habits—behavior patterns that are performed regularly. Some habits that are particularly important for Financial Life Planning are:

1. Your ability to maintain your focus on the task at hand

   a. For example, by delineating the steps necessary to be fully engaged in client meetings.

2. Maintaining consistency and clarity in your processes

   a. For example, in preparing for client meetings, I consistently review the client's file before meetings. I also make sure to spend a few minutes in silence to clear my head and become mentally prepared to bring the best of myself to each meeting.

3. Being open and non-judgmental

4. Listening empathetically and objectively

5. Returning client phone calls within twenty-four hours

6. Acknowledging jobs well done by colleagues, staff and clients

7. Taking care of your staff

   a. For example, through meetings, activities, holiday parties, trainings; by allowing each individual to express themselves fully; and by providing a consistent framework for them to work within.

8. Staying vigilant

   a. We all need to be constantly aware of opportunities, new knowledge, potential changes, or better methodologies or processes.

9. Constantly learning and raising the bar for yourself and others in your practice

   a. Yesterday's knowledge is not enough. Keep learning! We need to continue to "bring it" to our lives, businesses and clients every day.

10. Maintaining gratitude and respect for oneself and others

11. Self care: maintaining health and balance

Positioning yourself is a big task, but one that should be joyful and meaningful in many ways. After reading this section of the book, do you have an idea of what your current level of KASH is, and what you would like it to be? Address these points before moving on. This will bring you the confidence you need to position your business.

Positioning your Business:

Now that you have positioned yourself in terms of your KASH, it is time to think about what changes need to occur in your business to allow you to bring Financial Life Planning to your clients. Considering all you have done already, this is a relatively simple step. It's not like you are transitioning from being financial planner to becoming a florist. This is the time to ensure that the foundation of your business is strong and sound. Once again, clarity and consistency play an important role in the positioning process. For example, are your office processes and procedures documented and accurate? While this task might feel mundane, the benefits of having your structure, processes, and "how-to's" well thought out and in place will greatly add to your confidence and effectiveness.

In addition to increasing efficiency, clarity and consistency are vital in establishing and maintaining client relationships. For one thing, they help to build trust. Clients want and deserve a safe and stable environment in which to work with their advisors—after all, we are talking about nothing less than their money, their dreams and their future. You can demonstrate consistency in many ways, both large and small.

I remember several years ago, sitting in a car dealership waiting for service on my car. The guy next to me growled, "They used to serve coffee here in nice mugs and have nice pastries. Now they give you these lousy Styrofoam cups and crappy stale cookies. No wonder, their service has gone downhill, too!" I took his comments to heart. Any change that clients perceive as negative—regarding either your coffee or your financial acumen—can have a carryover effect on their confidence in you and your practice. Such changes can be upsetting, confusing and distracting. Through consistent behavior, you can give your clients what they expect and even exceed their expectations. Instead of putting out fires, you can revel in their delight.

The easiest way to achieve consistency is to clarify your processes. This means taking each process and detailing each step, sharing the process with your team, and then making sure it is followed rigorously. In my practice, we've standardized and documented the processes for everything from how our phones are answered to walking the client to the door at the end of a meeting. Consistency cuts down on unwanted surprises and system failures and creates an atmosphere of comfort and stability for the client.

This clarity and consistency also benefits your staff. Staff members thrive when they understand what they are expected to do. Furthermore, it allows them to address unexpected situations, which invariably will happen, with grace and wisdom, in a consistent and reliable manner. Finally, training new staff is simpler when your procedures are thoroughly and clearly codified.

Standardizing and documenting your office procedures is one way to position your business in order to integrate your new Financial Life Planning business model. In addition, you may also want to review these aspects of your business to see if they need modification:

- Articulate your mission statement in alignment with your philosophy.

- Redesign your website and marketing materials to reflect what you do and who you are.

- Meet with employees, colleagues and any other stakeholders. Be sure that they are on-board with the changes. When your entire team is following the same game plan, your operation will be cohesive and consistent, and you'll have created a platform for excellent communication, discussion and growth.

- Review the level of training and preparation necessary for each member of your staff. Ensure that everyone on your team is in the appropriate role and has the required training and skills. (For example, all advisors on our staff have attended the M.Q. Training, and many have attended the Kinder Training as well.)

- Establish a process for determining if new and existing clients are a good fit for your practice (see next chapter for more details).

- Ensure that your office environment reflects your vision.

- Incorporate life-planning elements into your meeting agendas.

Once you have addressed these points, I predict you will feel much more confident in your business model. You will know that your systems are sound, appropriate and well thought out. Of course, there will be more adjustments to make as you navigate these changes, but you will be much better prepared to deal with them.

Having prepared yourself and your business, you are now ready to open the doors and welcome your clients into your new and improved practice.

Positioning Your Clients:

"Do you just bring Life Planning to new clients and leave existing clients under the old method?"

This is one of the most common questions I am asked when speaking to planners about incorporating Life Planning into their practice. My response is always the same: "Why would I offer these opportunities only to new clients? Don't existing clients deserve my best services, too?"

I understand my colleagues' concern. They don't want their current clients to feel that they are moving in different directions. They're afraid they will undermine their clients' confidence in them. Basically, they're afraid it will look like they did a less than perfect job getting to know their clients from the beginning. I get it. I've been there. It's true that some clients may not be interested in changing the relationship. The point of positioning your clients is to determine which clients, both existing and new, are a good fit for your new business model and what you'll do if they aren't.

Before meeting with any clients, take some time to envision your target or ideal client. You may be surprised at how your target client is different now that you are incorporating Financial Life Planning. Consider the following:

1. Picture the clients you wish to work with and those you do not.

2. Determine the ideal characteristics of clients who fit into your new model.

3. Think of clients who might not react well to your change.

4. Can you understand why they might not react well? Can you imagine that some people will be resistant to opening themselves up to you?

5. If your answer to item 4 is "Yes," what actions you can take to help them make the transition to your new model—or how can you make the "letting go" process easier for them and for you?

The truth is, not everyone will embrace your ideas with your level of excitement. Some people are more open to change than others, and that's just the way it is. Every business is different, so determining your ideal client will help you begin to understand which of your current clients are a good fit and how to deal with the ones who are not.

Another aspect of client positioning is to consider the financial ramifications. Implementing life-planning means spending additional time with clients and in the planning process. Some of our clients with the financial resources to pay for our services didn't have the time or interest necessary to invest in this process. Other clients who were very excited about the process would have a harder time affording our fees. We had always included a certain percentage of *pro bono* cases in our firm, and we adapted our business plan to these realities.

There is no blueprint for every situation. You will have to figure out for yourself what will work for you on a case-by-case method. You may imagine how clients will react to the change. You may feel some fear of losing clients or revenue. The key, once again, is clarity. If you're clear, you can more easily accept where your clients are coming from and deal with them honestly, kindly and respectfully. If you know why you are doing what you are doing, it makes it easier to accept that some clients just will not be right for your process or your practice.

When I made the shift in my own business, I was keenly aware that not all of my clients would be a good fit for Life Planning. Still, I was very attached to some of these clients, for emotional and financial reasons. Some were people I'd had relationships with for many years whom I knew wouldn't engage with the Life Planning exercises. A few clients looked at the Kinder questions and wouldn't even answer them. Some of them were in survival mode, some were cynical and others just wouldn't engage. My associates and I all dealt with clients who said things like "Don't talk to me about this stuff; just manage my investments." We tried to introduce them gently and remain non-judgmental to their responses. Over time, we gained clarity about how to deal with each case. We decided to remain flexible. Even now, I don't have life plans for every single one of my clients, and I'm still able to offer them excellent financial planning advice. For other clients, it made more sense to help them transfer to an affiliated firm that was more than grateful for the business.

In the same way that some clients were obviously a great fit for our new model, other clients very obviously were not. The shift in our practice actually gave us the opportunity to do some much needed house cleaning. In assessing our new business model, my colleagues and I agreed that mutual respect was an essential component of a healthy working relationship. Therefore, if a client displayed behaviors that were inconsistent with that base line, we would release them from our practice. Here are some of the behaviors we decided we would no longer accept from clients:

- Abusive behavior: any client who is verbally abusive to an advisor or a staff person

- Disrespect for time: any client who frequently cancels appointments at the last minute without a reasonable excuse, or does not return phone calls or emails

- Disrespect for advice: any client who seeks our advice and consistently disregards that advice, even after realizing poor results

- Disregard for professional services: any client who provides poor information without regard for our time and effort and is unwilling to pay a reasonable fee for extra work

Making the necessary decisions about whom you will serve is not always easy. That being said, it is essential for your success, as well as your clients'. It is perfectly acceptable to acknowledge that you have a limited amount of time and resources available and you have the right and obligation to work with those who fit best with your practice, staff and values. I don't want you to panic that on the day you decide to change your practice, you are going to immediately dismiss this group of non-aligning clients. It's a process and it takes time, consideration and proper positioning. It may sound scary, but as you move into the process you will find ease and confidence because you are conducting your practice the right way, for the right reasons.

Now that you have prepared yourself, it's time to present your existing clients with the changes in your practice. Here is a checklist to guide you through the process.

1. Send an announcement of the changes you're making to the practice. Invite clients to come in for a meeting.

2. If the client does not respond to the announcement, call them directly. Be prepared to explain why you have made changes and how excited you are to share this information with them.

3. Set up the meeting. At the meeting, introduce the reasons behind the changes.

4. Discuss any fee changes if you have decided to change your fee structure.

5. Introduce a Life Planning exercise and have clients practice it.

6. After they have experienced an exercise (or two), prepare to listen empathetically. Ask questions that clarify their comments, without judgment. For example, the question we typically ask after an exercise is, "How was that for you?" Be prepared to learn more about your client than you thought possible.

7. During the meeting, be mindful of your clients' body language. What are they telling you with their posture, their arm and body position? Are they positive and open or distant and reserved?

8. Notice and observe your own body language.

9. Notice how your clients respond to the questions. Are they defensive or are they forthcoming? How well do they engage in conversation? Are they trusting, or do they seem secretive and closed? If you are seeing, feeling and hearing resistance, I suggest you "announce the elephant" by simply asking, "It seems you are experiencing some resistance or difficulty. Would you care to talk about it?" If the client is shut down and refuses to go forward, then you must determine how much effort you wish to devote, or if other options are more appropriate, such as trying to re-engage at another time.

Observe your own responses. There needs to be mindfulness on all sides. Are your responses well thought out? Is the focus remaining on the client? Are you asking more than telling, and listening more than talking? As you begin to meet with your existing clients and present your new process, you will find that typically your clients will fall into two broad categories: those who love it immediately and those who are resistant. The resistant ones seem to fit into two sub-categories: those who just need more time to adjust and feel comfortable, and those who will never be able or willing to change their level of openness with you. If you meet with resistance initially, ask questions that allow them to talk about their experience. For example, we ask, "How was that for you? What did you get from that exercise?" Reiterate your reasons for change, and explain why this process is in their best interest. Then try again at your next meeting. If the resistance continues, you may need to communicate your beliefs more clearly and offer the choice to migrate to another planner and firm.

When both advisor and client are committed to the process, Life Planning is a hugely enjoyable, energizing, and fulfilling experience for both parties. However, those clients who kick and scream through the whole process will only be an energy and resource drain for you and your staff. The point of incorporating Financial Life Planning into your practice is to know your clients so well that you can build a plan that truly resonates with their values, dreams and goals. If the client is not willing to divulge enough information to allow you to know them, then how can you do effective and meaningful planning?

The question then becomes: should you be working with those who are not aligned or who are unwilling to provide that access? In my business, we have determined that we generally will not. This was a difficult leap of faith at first. The fear arose, What if *everyone* is resistant? There will be no business! We soon discovered that, although understandable, we were just feeling the irrational fear of the unknown. We took the plunge with the confidence and excitement generated from proper positioning, and the transition for both our staff and clients was therefore surprisingly smooth.

In the next chapter, I will discuss the process for bringing new clients into your practice. Now, let's recap for a moment. At this point, you have envisioned your preferred future and created action steps to move yourself and your practice from thought to action. You have examined your skill sets and weaknesses and assessed the knowledge and skills that you need to acquire. You have examined your personal integrity to ensure that you are moving in a direction that is harmonious with your values. You have spoken with associates and colleagues about the shift in your business. You have ensured that your staff training, foundational systems and infrastructure are effective and in alignment with your new practices. Your website and marketing materials reflect who you are and what you do with clarity. You have made wonderful and meaningful progress!

Here you are, confident and in position to change your approach to financial planning in ways that benefit you, your team, and your clients. You have looked inside and prepared yourself and your business for change. Now it is time to manifest these changes and share your new improved practice with the world. Success, as defined by you, awaits. Allow me to reframe. Success is certainly here, right now! You have made enormous progress and have done a vast amount of great work to get here. Can you take a moment or two to celebrate your many wonderful successes in navigating the trail thus far? Please do! I highly recommend a whole lot of savoring and celebrating; you deserve it.

Part Three:
Outside

Chapter Nine

Is it a Fit?

"The shoe that fits one person pinches another; there is no recipe for living that suits all cases."

~ Carl Gustav Jung

In a few minutes, I will be meeting with Joan and Pete, potential new clients who've been referred to me by their CPA. I want to focus completely on the clients during our meeting, so I turn off my computer and phones, review my notes and take a few moments to clear my mind.

Joan and Pete are both in their 50s. Pete is an executive with a Fortune 500 firm and Joan is a self-employed designer; they have two children, one in college and the other in high school. They have never worked with a planner but have had a relationship with a stockbroker for the last ten years and feel they have been burned by poor advice and worse performance. They're coming to my office today because their CPA advised them that they might benefit from working with someone who will utilize a holistic approach to financial planning. The fact that they agreed to meet with me indicates that they're probably open to learning a new way of managing their finances.

This is the moment you've been waiting for. After all of your hard work, you are ready to welcome your potential clients and demonstrate the power of Financial Life Planning. I call the first meeting with a prospective client a Fit meeting.

The Fit meeting is the time to introduce clients to your Financial Life Planning model. Most importantly, it is an exploratory meeting to determine whether there is good chemistry and sufficient reason to engage in the very personal process of Financial Life Planning. In order to assess whether there is a proper basis for moving forward, the Fit meeting is necessary and important for everyone at the table. Both planner and client need to understand each other's expectations, processes, needs and desired outcomes in order for the relationship to be mutually productive and fulfilling.

When we are working with a couple, both parties must attend and be active participants in the creation and manifestation of their financial goals. Each individual has his or her own experience, ideas, fears, desires and dreams regarding their financial situation. Each partner must be respected and their needs integrated into the creation of their plan. At this early stage of your relationship, you want to show your clients that you recognize that each individual has their own attitude about what they want their financial life to look like. You also want to demonstrate your ability to integrate each of their sometimes divergent needs into a collective whole.

This first meeting is your chance to wow your new clients. Don't underestimate the wow-factor! You have the opportunity to provide a new experience, one that is comforting, empowering and motivating. The wow-factor is the impression you give a potential client so their experience is positive, different and impactful. It begins with their very first contact with you and your staff.

> Pete and Joan enter our offices at 10:00 on a rainy Thursday morning. As soon as they step through the door, my receptionist, Ashley, pops out from behind her desk and with a smile, greets them and takes their coats. "You must be Mr. and Mrs. Johnson. I am Ashley; we spoke on the phone yesterday to confirm your appointment. May I offer you a beverage? Michael will be with you shortly."
>
> Ashley returns with the beverages and ushers them into the conference room, which she has already set up in accordance

with our office procedures. I hear the door close and enter from the second entrance. "Welcome. My name is Michael Kay; it's great to meet you both. Is there anything you need before we get started?"

Even though they are smiling, I notice tension in their jaws and faces. Their smiles are tight, and there's a level of anxiety in their voices. My job is to try and put them at ease during our time together.

The stage has been set. Now it's time for you to demonstrate that you have the necessary ability, passion and skills while assessing whether the clients are right for your practice. This might sound like a lot to accomplish in one hour, and it is—but it can and must be done. Let's take a closer look at the Fit meeting by examining each of its steps.

The Fit Meeting Process:

1. Set the tone for an open exchange.

2. Demonstrate why and how you differentiate yourself from other planners.

3. Discuss expectations.

4. Promote interdependency between client and planner.

5. Demystify the financial planning process.

6. Initiate the assessment period.

7. Wrap up.

8. Decide how to move forward.

1. Set the tone for open exchange.

Imagine yourself in your conference room, sitting next to your prospective client. (Note that I did not say "across." I prefer to sit next to my clients without a table top between us; this approach is more welcoming and accessible; it sends the message that we are collaborating as a team.)

You've never met this person before and your objective is to help them feel at ease as well as bring them into alignment with your firm's practice model. Where do you begin?

Once Joan and Pete are settled, I ask whether they have any time constraints that day. I explain that these meetings generally last about an hour to an hour and thirty minutes, depending on their questions, and ask if that's all right. I can see the ice melting a bit as they ease further into their chairs. "In front of you is a basic agenda we use during our initial Fit meetings," I say, motioning towards the folders on the table. "Let's take a moment to review."

The first item on the agenda is "HBQs" or Hot Burning Questions. "Many people, when they first come to visit with us, have a list of questions they would like to address. I want to make sure we uncover those questions first so they don't get lost. Are there any questions you'd like to make sure we review before the end of our meeting today?"

Joan takes out a sheet of paper from her briefcase. They've obviously spent time in preparation for this meeting. I write their questions on a whiteboard as she reads them off their list. Their questions center on our process, fee structure, background and qualifications. They also have a few questions about their retirement plan and current financial situation. Once I have recorded them all, I sit back down. "I will address all of these questions before our meeting ends."

They look at each other. "Okay," Pete says, with a shrug.

"I want to acknowledge that this can be a little stressful at first. However, I urge you to be open and direct regarding any and all questions or concerns you might have. My job is not to judge you in any way, but to act as a facilitator and coach. In fact, we consider our conference room to be sacred space. Therefore, whatever you say here is safe from criticism. The ground rules are simple: in discussions, each party is responsible for listening without judg-

ment in order to seek to understand the other. Any questions?"
Pete and Joan both shake their heads.

"Okay. Let me ask you a question. What do you want to be when you grow up?"

Pete laughs out loud. Hands interlaced behind his head, he leans back in his chair and says, "I've always wanted to be my own boss."

Joan's spine stiffens. "Really?" she asks.

"I mean, I don't know if it's possible; there are so many obstacles, and besides, I am not even sure that I would know what to do," Pete responds, a hint of guilt in his voice.

I lean forward, looking at them both. "It looks like there are a great many things to talk about. Are you ready to get started?"

"We're ready," Joan says firmly.

Joan and Pete arrived with few expectations but a good deal of anxiety. They had no framework for this meeting and were prepared to be skeptical and reserved. Within the first five minutes, they were shown respect for their time, consideration for their questions and that my team was organized and prepared to address their needs. By explaining the purpose of our meeting and how I expected to communicate, the door was opened for comfortable exchange.

Many clients, especially those who have never worked with a planner, feel somewhat anxious when meeting a new planner. It is safe to say that many people are reticent to share personal and financial information, let alone their dreams and goals, with someone they do not know. Opening up can be frightening, especially when it may shed light on things that need to change. Some clients open up very quickly; with others it may take a bit more time. The Fit meeting provides you with your first and greatest opportunity to create a safe environment, thereby allowing clients to communicate with greater ease.

One of the most effective ways to help your clients feel safe is to convey that you are not judging them and that you are there to help them get from their current position to one that is closer to their ideal. I cannot reinforce enough that as the planner, you must leave your opinions and judgments at the door and not bring them into the meeting with you. By speaking clearly, respectfully and without judgment, you make it easier for your clients to share the information you will need to help them.

Beginning a Fit meeting on a decisive and positive note sets the tone for the meeting and indeed the relationship. The more you demonstrate active interest in learning about your clients and understanding who they are, the more it is apparent that you are attuned to their needs.

2. Demonstrate why and how you differentiate yourselves from other planners.

*The next item on the Agenda is to offer a sample of Financial Life Planning. Before doing this, I take a few moments to **briefly** explain my own journey in adapting my practice to include Life Planning. Joan and Pete both smile as I describe the benefits this shift has brought my clients, my business, and me personally. I emphasize that my objective as a Financial Life Planner is to help people articulate their values, dreams, and financial musts—those things that must happen in order for them to feel successful.*

"In order for us to get to know you beyond the numbers, we utilize some exercises," I explain. "The first exercise that I will ask you to complete is called the Financial Satisfaction Survey [see appendix]. The questions in this survey focus on your level of satisfaction right now in a broad range of financial areas. Please take a few minutes and fill in the form. You'll notice that each of you has your own form in your folder. It's important that you do this independently."

I watch closely as they fill out the forms. They are truly thinking about their answers and I'm excited to see their responses. I wait until they're both finished then collect the worksheets and take them out to Ashley so she can make copies. They look at each other, probably wondering what the other has recorded.

While we wait for the copies, I sit back down and ask, "How was that for you?"

"I guess I feel good about some things and not so good about others," Pete says tentatively. Joan nods in agreement. Ashley returns with the forms and I distribute them again, retaining the copies. Scanning their worksheets, I search for indications of strengths or perceived weaknesses. Contrary to what they may expect, I lead with the strengths.

"Pete, you ranked your level of satisfaction with your company benefits, retirement nest egg and ability to provide for your family very highly. That's seems like a great accomplishment. Tell me more."

Pete sits back, eyes opened wide. "It makes me feel very proud to have reached this level of income to provide for my family. Growing up, I never imagined I would ever come close to making this much money or experiencing this level of financial success. It still doesn't seem real to me." His words hang in the air and the room is quiet. Joan sits gazing at her husband, obviously moved. "I never knew you felt that way, Pete. That is so wonderful. You've done such an amazing job, and you should feel proud." I sit back and relish the moment being shared between them.

Here and now is the opportunity to express your excitement about Financial Life Planning and its impact on people's lives. Make it crystal clear that your objective is to help them articulate and work towards living their dreams, and that their Financial Life Plan is the roadmap to that success. In order to make this concept real for your clients, you must believe completely in the efficacy of your methods. *Your level of success is directly related to your level of belief.*

Since one objective of this meeting is to build trust, it's important for you to demonstrate openness by speaking candidly about your practice and why you do what you do. There's a fine line here: you don't want to talk about yourself too much. Your client is not paying to hear about the twelve deer you killed with a slingshot on your last hunting trip. However, they do need to know that you are not only qualified but passionate about what you are able to offer them.

Next comes the experiential segment of the meeting. You give your clients an exercise so that they can directly experience how you operate. After working through the exercise, you solicit their comments and reactions. Then, you demonstrate that you have heard and understood what they are saying. Three steps are the crux of this exploratory process: Experience, Discuss, Understand. Let's look at each step a little more closely.

Experience: As educators know, providing an experience is much more powerful than simply giving an explanation. The experience makes it real rather than theoretical. Typically, I will integrate one or two experiential exercises into this part of the meeting, depending on time and client response.

Discuss: After they have completed their first Financial Life Planning exercises, I provide clients with an opportunity to elaborate on their answers and reactions to the exercises. The intention is to get clients engaged in the process so they will feel comfortable communicating their thoughts and ideas.

Understand: After the client has completed an exercise and we've had meaningful discussion, I repeat back to the client what I've heard them say. This allows the client to feel heard, and it also gives me the opportunity to fit the new information into the larger context of what is necessary for the creation of the plan. For example, if a client discusses the importance of a financial legacy as a cornerstone to their satisfaction, then that information must be properly weighted when I create their plan.

Applying exercises at the Fit meeting will give you information about the client and their values as well as their level of openness, their communication patterns and how they process information. In most cases, this process elicits incredibly rich conversation and a sense of positive anticipation. Wow! For the first time, someone is actually asking the client to talk about their thoughts and feelings—about their life! Talk about positive energy in the room! But be aware, there might be some clients for whom this conversation evokes a negative or defeatist attitude. Do not panic. You are the voice of reason. As Lao Tzu said, "The journey of a thousand miles begins with a single step." Remind your clients that together, you will co-create a path to improvement. The more you reassure and show belief in your clients, the more motivated they will be to move through transitions and change.

3. Discuss expectations.

It is essential to discuss expectations very early in the process, and definitely before you agree to work together. Planners need to know what the clients expect of them so they can meet and ideally exceed their expectations. Clients need to know what will be expected of them throughout the process and where the planner's responsibility lies. We want our clients to be satisfied with our services and to feel we are attentive to their needs. However, if we are asked to go beyond our normal scope, we must be compensated accordingly. Establishing expectations from both perspectives allows you to assess whether this relationship is a good fit for you and your practice.

We all know that unspoken expectations can create future problems, confusion and a crisis of trust. Such confusion, and the disappointment that inherently results, will not support your desire to have long-term clients who become your strongest advocates. Can you think of a situation where unspoken expectations led to a problem? Can you think of a situation where excellent communications created excellent relationships? Take a few minutes and consider these two experiences.

Several years ago, during a discussion with a prospective client, he told me that he expected me to translate data in a specific format for his use. I explained that our software would not allow us to do so and that if it was that important, we would have to be compensated for the additional time it would take to convert the data. In a very short amount of time, we were able to create a strategy that worked for both of us, laying the ground for clear and successful communications.

Clarifying expectations is vital in terms of the client's satisfaction, future introductions and creating a financial relationship that reflects a win/win interaction. For example, if you find out after you have proposed a fee that the client expects more meetings, more communications or more analysis than normal, you will be on the wrong side of the financial transaction. No doubt, this will leave you dissatisfied in the relationship. It is your responsibility to ask the right questions and make sure that you understand the clients' responses.

After completing and discussing the Life Planning exercise, Joan and Pete's demeanor is completely different than when they first arrived. They are obviously engaged in the process and exhibit a great deal of enthusiasm. Now it's time to ask what may be the most important question of this meeting.

"Tell me, Joan, Pete—if we agree to work together, what do you expect from us to make this a great and lasting relationship?"

My question obviously surprises them. After thinking awhile, Joan answers, "A great relationship would require honesty, integrity, excellent communications and certainly top notch expertise. Yes, those attributes would definitely make me happy!"

Pete follows up quickly. "Proactive, absolutely proactive. You know how busy we are—we need to make sure that whomever we work with will take the initiative and bring issues to us that need to be considered. I mean, I don't have the time or expertise to think of everything; that's why we want an advisor, to give us good sound advice on a proactive basis!"

"Is there anything else you can think of?" I ask. "Take a minute or two to make sure there is nothing we have forgotten or need to revisit."

"No, I think that's about it. Timely, proactive, thoughtful, communicative and high integrity. Yes, that covers it," Pete concludes.

I give it a minute to see if either of them has anything else to say. At this time I am just listening and only comment if I need clarification. Unless I know right away that we can't meet their expectations, I won't make any commitment to do so until I've had a chance to think it through and potentially check it with other members of my team. "Good," I respond. "Now, I need to tell you what we expect from you."

Pete and Joan listen intently as I outline my firm's expectations for excellent client relationships. I then run down the list of what they can expect from us. Again, their response is overwhelmingly positive.

The first thing I want to do is make sure that I understand the client's expectations. I want to keep the focus on the client and what they care about for as long as possible before shifting to what we expect from the relationship. The reason is so that the client has as much time as necessary to explain, discuss and articulate what they care about. It's that understanding that will help me know if we can meet their expectations and what their points of view and thought process is.

It may seem obvious, but it's still important to discuss what we expect from our clients:

1. We expect the client to provide correct information on a timely basis.

2. We expect the client to ask questions when they arise.

3. We expect the client to let us know if their situation or thinking changes.

4. We expect the client to make and keep timely appointments, unless there are extraordinary situations.

5. We expect the client to review our output on a timely basis and to sign off on their assent.

6. We expect them to live up to our financial agreement.

At the same time, there are some basic practices that our clients can expect from us:

1. We will act with integrity.

2. All client information is held in confidence.

3. We will bring our best skills to the table and will be fully present for them during meetings and whenever we are working on their plans. They will have our undivided attention.

4. We will work with our clients in accordance with the CFP Board of Standards requirements. These standards cover professional ethics, standards and duties. We will go beyond what is required to provide an extraordinary experience that incorporates the principles of Life Planning.

5. We will continue to hone our skills and knowledge for the benefit of our clients.

6. We will return phone calls within a stated period of time.

7. A client can expect that our fees will be reasonable in relationship to the work performed.

Another critical aspect of defining expectations is delineating how we will communicate and work together. I always ask how the client prefers to communicate regarding routine matters: by email, phone, letter, or face-to-face meetings. There might be some communications that should only be done in person and some information that can be readily exchanged via email. It is important to agree at the beginning of the relationship on what is appropriate and most effective.

Finally, during this expectation segment I define our boundaries. There are things we will not or cannot do, such as serving as a psychologist, therapist, tax attorney, CPA or perform any function that is not appropriate to our role. If issues arise that are beyond our scope, we offer referrals.

4. Promote interdependency between client and planner.

It's time to introduce Joan and Pete to Jim, the Junior Planner who will be gathering, filtering and recording the quantitative aspects of their plan. After making introductions, I explain that

we are most productive when all parties agree to work interde-
pendently. "The client must provide solid data. The flip side is
also true: you need to hear from us on a timely basis if infor-
mation is missing or we have any questions. Does that make
sense?" Pete and Joan understand this clearly.

I thank Jim, and he leaves us to continue our meeting. [There
are times when the Junior Planner will attend the entire Fit
meeting, depending on time available.] "There is another as-
pect of interdependency that I want to discuss with you now.
Our goal here is to build a plan around your values and your
financial musts; we want to understand what must happen in
your life for you to feel satisfied and successful. In order for this
to be the case, our conversations need to be open and honest.
For example, attitudes about money are typically rooted in our
history. Unless we understand those roots, it is difficult to create
a plan that might involve changing any limiting behaviors. We
are dependent on each other's forthrightness to produce a plan
that is uniquely yours. Does that make sense?" Joan and Pete
look at each other and seem to take this in. After a moment,
they look back at me and nod in agreement.

It is vital that your client comes away from this meeting knowing that
this is a collaborative, interdependent partnership that requires both parties to act in concert with each other. There is an essential give and take of
information that is necessary to create, build and integrate a life plan that
addresses the unique needs of each client. When this interdependency is
well established, the client takes ownership and is more likely to respond
and implement changes because the plan is theirs. This is when the perfect synthesis of knowledge occurs: the client is able to articulate their
values, and the life planner is then able to mesh the quantitative information with the qualitative to co-create a plan that has meaning to the client.
This understanding cannot be accomplished without both parties' active
involvement.

5. Demystify the financial planning process.

"Okay, I get that we have a lot to talk about. How do we go about this?" Joan asks. "We're busy people, so how soon can we expect to have a plan in place?"

"Great question, Joan. In order to create a meaningful Financial Life Plan, we examine three aspects of your financial situation: the first is your current financial condition; second, we examine your past history with money and money messages, including money habits. Finally, we will discuss your vision for your ideal future. Here's how we'll go about it. The first step is for you to provide us with some preliminary data. We will give you a checklist and request that you gather the required information and send it back within a mutually agreed upon time frame. After that, within one week, we will quote you a fee for our services. Once you have reviewed and accepted our proposal, you sign a financial planning letter of agreement. After the agreement is signed, we'll provide you with a list of additional information that we will need to work on the quantitative side of the plan. You will be working with Jim, whom you met earlier, on this portion of your plan. I will keep my focus on the Life Planning aspects. Any questions so far?"

"How long does this normally take, Michael?" Pete asks.

"It depends on how quickly you deliver the needed information, which must be both accurate and concise. Once we receive the information we need, we prepare a preliminary draft of a financial plan. That draft will contain two schedules: one is net worth and the other cash flow. At this point, we need to ensure that the data is correct; otherwise, the plan would be built on inaccurate numbers. The next step is for you to review it and sign off on its accuracy. Any questions?"

"I get it. It's just like sending my clients the first draft of their design," Joan says.

"That's right. As you can see, we each have a role to play in producing your plan, and it's vital that we work interdependently." I pause to allow my words to sink in. "The Life Planning materials enable me to understand what motivates you—what you care most about—and potential blocks or obstacles, so that your plan is built on the integrity of your core values and is realistic. We evaluate the data and create scenarios in order to find out if you are working towards your goals effectively or whether modifications are necessary. Do you have any questions?"

Joan looks at Pete and then at me. "Amazingly enough, no. For the first time, I think I actually get what it is that you do."

One of the reasons financial plans can seem overwhelming is that sometimes they are! Financial planning clients can feel that they are being confronted with something they do not understand. Your obligation is to explain clearly what is being done and why, and to remind your clients that all the questions and exercises tie into their ultimate goal. We explain our process, timelines and who will be involved in the process so that the client understands what goes into the co-creation of their plan. It also demonstrates where and when their direct involvement is critical. When you establish reasonable timelines, you provide clients with a picture of how and when the process will unfold and therefore when they can expect a completed plan. Clients are more likely to respond quickly when they understand the process and their roles in that process. Similarly, the more quickly you demonstrate that the process is transparent and communication is open, the sooner information will flow.

6. Initiate the assessment period.

"Well, you two, we've covered a great deal today. There is one more thing to discuss. There's been a lot of information shared today and we all need time to digest what we've heard. Because of this, it is our policy to initiate an assessment period before agreeing to an engagement. This gives us both time to ask clarifying questions and make a decision about working together. That being said, I propose that you go home, talk about today's experience, call or email me if you have any ad-

ditional questions, and then we'll talk Monday morning about what we've concluded in terms of moving ahead. How does this sound to you?"

They look at me in surprise. "Does that mean you might not agree to work with us?" Joan asks.

"That's a good question. The fact is, I need to think about your expectations, our schedule, and our ability to meet your needs and whether I believe we can create an ideal working relationship within the scope of our firm. There are cases where it just doesn't work. In cases like that, I will refer the person out to another firm we know and trust."

They both look a little distressed. "Hmm, I was feeling very good about this, and now I am a little concerned," Pete says.

"The saw cuts in both directions, Pete. You two might leave here and decide that I am just not a good fit for you and your situation, in which case I would expect you to tell me so, openly and directly. It is rare that we do not engage clients who wish to work with us, but it has happened. I just want you to be aware of our process. It is nothing to worry about. From my perspective, today has been extraordinary!"

With this statement, Pete and Joan are both relieved. We agree that Pete will call me on Monday morning.

Is it better to be a minute too fast or an hour too slow? In this case, being too slow is beneficial. You may wonder why we build an assessment period into the Financial Life Planning process, because it appears to slow the momentum of enlisting new clients. Here's why: an assessment period benefits both parties by allowing them to integrate and understand what they've heard. This separation allows each party to "sleep on it" before committing their time, energy and resources. In addition, there is a great danger in trying to close the deal too fast. People don't want to be pushed. If you rush to decision after spending all this time trying to get them comfortable, they may feel pressured. A hasty decision can also encumber you with a relationship that you are not well suited to handle. Have you ever heard of someone who went on vacation and came back owning a time-share? While some people might be truly excited about such a purchase, others experience buyers' remorse at having made a decision when they felt pressured or overwhelmed by the "once-in-a-lifetime" deal being offered.

There is the additional benefit of appearing exclusive. Your client feels special in that they have been selected; this conveys that you won't accept just anyone who can fog a mirror. You want your clients to feel that working with you is special, and you want them to want to be selected. This process will enhance your reputation with your clients; those you bring into the practice will feel good because they qualified. Everyone likes to qualify! It will add to their confidence, demonstrate that you are selective and caring, and provide them with an experience that is unique, special and centered around their needs. The assessment period allows for that feeling of exclusivity.

7. Wrap up.

An hour and fifteen minutes have elapsed since Joan and Pete entered the conference room. Their coffee cups are empty and their note pads full. Our discussion was candid and forthright, as I'd expect from a business executive and a business owner. A dynamic spark of enthusiasm crackles in the air.

I ask if are there any questions that still need to be answered. They both shake their heads. "To be honest, we came here today full of anxiety, and we're leaving today feeling like we found a new friend!" Joan says. I walk them into the reception area, help them with their coats and escort them to the door. "We'll get back to you on Monday," Joan states.

"Looking forward to it. Have a great weekend, and please don't hesitate to get in touch if you have any questions."

As soon as they leave, I return to the conference room and review my notes from our meeting. I summarize the notes so they can be rendered into an email that I will send them later today. Next, I talk to the appropriate members of the planning team to get their thoughts, especially pertaining to timing and areas of specific expertise. Joan and Pete are working with a fairly short timeline, and I must make sure we have the ability to perform as requested.

It was a great meeting, and I'm very pleased. I already have lots of ideas about how to move forward, but the assessment period is there for me as well.

8. Decide how to move forward.

The objective of the Fit meeting is to create a foundation of openness that will help both parties decide whether or not to engage. There are four possible outcomes: 1) both parties agree to work together; 2) the client does not wish to proceed; 3) the planner does not wish to proceed; 4) neither party wishes to proceed.

In the first case, you're both off and running and the process begins. In the case of Joan and Pete, I heard from Pete Monday morning, and we agreed that we were all ready to work together. Our next meeting was incredibly productive because of the foundation of trust and understanding established at the Fit meeting.

The last scenario where neither party wishes to proceed is easy as well; both disengage and go their separate ways. No harm, no foul. Where it gets sticky is when one of you wants to move forward and the other doesn't. If the client does not wish to continue, it is certainly appropriate to ask them to share their reasons and thereby allow you to understand their thinking. Sometimes it has nothing to do with you as a planner; it may be that they are not quite ready to get started, and there's a chance they will reengage in the future. If the reason is because they did not feel comfortable with you or that your methods weren't what they were looking for, you can certainly ask if there was anything specific that was a deal-breaker. The differences between their needs and your offering will help you understand why they believe it was not a good fit.

What happens if, after meeting with a client, you do not believe it is the right relationship for you to pursue? How do you handle the situation where you feel that "no" is the best answer? Admittedly, this is difficult. There have been several times where I arrived at that decision. The challenge is to communicate it in such a way that is kind, respectful and direct.

First, understand why you've come to that conclusion. Is it a personality clash? A gut feeling? It is essential that you come to the conversation with a clear understanding of why this relationship is not a good fit for you. Otherwise, you might find yourself in the middle of a negotiation or backpedaling, which in the final analysis is not what you want. Saying "yes" when "no" is the right answer will create poor relationships and internal dissatisfaction. Relationships must be solid "win/win" scenarios in order for both parties to feel satisfied. A "win/lose" situation does not work! Explain to the prospect that you enjoyed meeting them but after consideration, you have concluded that you do not believe you can meet their expectations and therefore are not able to create an ongoing relationship at this time. I think it is also important to offer them a referral to another planner that you respect. For some great pointers on this topic, I suggest reading William Ury's book, *The Power of a Positive No,* or Patti Breitman and Connie Hatch's work, *How to Say No Without Feeling Guilty.*

Your objective is to build a practice comprised of clients with whom you are excited to work. In utilizing a Fit process, you create a systematic method for determining who those people are and who they aren't. By the end of this process, both you and your clients are ready and enthusiastic about moving forward together. All in all, it fits!

Chapter Ten

Data Gathering

"In order to truly know each other, it is indispensable to know how to listen to each other, and above all to want to listen to each other."

~ Enrico Bruschini, Art Historian

The financial planning letter of agreement has been signed. The engagement is a go. You have explained the basics of Financial Life Planning and have learned a bit about your client through the tools utilized in the Fit meeting. You and your client have established a timeline that will serve as a guide in moving the process to completion. The next step is to accumulate sufficient information to understand your client, both from a numbers or quantitative perspective and from the qualitative aspect of understanding their current situation as well as their goals, dreams and financial musts. This process involves looking forward to the possibilities, challenges and dreams that are most important to their satisfaction. You cannot effectively plan for the future, though, until you have taken a good look at the past. Some of the data most integral to your clients' ongoing success lies in their own history with money and goal setting. As an advisor, your job is to ask the right questions to help your clients provide you with the information you will need in order to create the right plan for them.

The primary focus of this chapter will be gathering qualitative data. Of course, the quantitative information is vital as well. As a Financial Life Planner, you are always cognizant of the numbers, which are relatively easy to come by. Most people who come to a financial planner expect to divulge this kind of information. More challenging is to uncover the thoughts, habits, and emotions that control your clients' relationship with money and to understand them from the context of their present, past, and future. As a Life Planner, is it vital to discover your clients' past history with money and the "money scripts"[14] they have brought with them from childhood into adulthood. You also need to have a keen understanding of their dreams and goals for the present and future. This investigation is at the heart of data gathering.

Some traditional planners might consider this a waste of time or a non-essential; however, nothing could be further from the truth. Consider this quote from George Kinder: "For all of us, the purpose of goal work is to resolve the apparent conflict between life and money and to decide where each of us needs to be. We have to locate the source of our own integrity, determine what the dream of freedom means to us, and decide how to move toward it. This is hard, demanding work. But if we fail to explore and articulate our goals, we will not so much lead our lives as find ourselves trapped in a hell of confusion, frustration, and purposeless acquisition."[15]

Qualitative data gathering allows the planner to understand the client on a level much deeper than the numbers alone, deeper than merely asking about their goals. Hearing the clients articulate what's vital to them, what concerns them, and what they need to feel good about or become better prepared for, allows the advisor to construct a plan around their values, dreams and needs.

Data gathering can typically be accomplished in one or two meetings, depending on the client's level of clarity, openness and the degree of work done to prepare for the discussions. We typically ask that the more challenging and time-consuming exercises be completed at home, with minimal distractions. If proper time and focus have been invested, it makes the discussions more fruitful and more time efficient. If the client is unwilling or unable to access this information and share it openly, the process is elongated and more time will be needed to gain appropriate understanding in order to build the plan. We do not want to overwhelm clients with too much intense introspection, yet we cannot allow too much time to go by without moving the process forward. It's your job to keep clients motivated and set an appropriate pace and reasonable expectations.

It's also your job to stay even-keeled and supportive as your clients open up to you. As I've said numerous times already, your active, empathetic listening is crucial. Remember that your job is simply to be with the client during moments of emotional turmoil; it is not your job to fix it or provide therapy or counseling. Meaningful bonds are created when you accept your clients without judgment and allow them to assimilate their responses and feelings without offering advice or suggestions. It can be tempting to jump in with my own sage advice, yet the bonding that results from keeping my mouth shut is generally much more effective! Each time I make the decision to listen with acceptance instead of giving advice, the result is a closer relationship with my client, who is then more apt to share openly because the experience has been positive.

There are three main components to qualitative data gathering: looking at the present, the past and the future. The order in which you conduct your investigation is vital. The present tells you what is, the past shows, in most cases, why the present is the way it is, and your inquiry into the future provides a target to build towards.

In the Fit meeting, you collected a certain amount of information about your client to give you a sense of how to take the next steps. In order to really understand your clients, and in order for their plan to be a success, you have to look deeper still.

Looking at the Present:

Think of a doctor diagnosing a patient. The doctor's first questions are likely to be, "How are you feeling today? What symptoms, aches, or pains are you experiencing? What's going on?" All of these are important questions in the quest for a proper diagnosis. Next, the physician is going to look at the patient's history: what illnesses, diseases or problems occurred in the past for the patient and the patient's family. Once a diagnosis has been made, based on the patient's present symptoms and past history, the doctor can provide strategies for an improved future.

The Financial Life Planner works in pretty much the same way. We first assess where the client is in the moment. We then look to the past for clues as to how the client got here and what kinds of strategies will be most effective. We elicit information about the client's preferred future so we can map out a clear, precise plan that takes all the information into account.

Qualitative data gathering in the present is all about understanding a client's level of satisfaction with their current life and situation. It is the jumping-off point from which to understand the client's current thinking, financial well-being and attitude. In working with clients to create a future that aligns with their own unique dreams, we begin with the Wheel of Life exercise (see appendix). This exercise, based on a common coaching exercise, was adapted by Money Quotient to help a client graphically depict their current satisfaction regarding their Financial Life, Personal Health, Home, Family, Inner Growth, Leisure, Community, Work Life and Learning. By completing their Wheel of Life, clients can see the areas in their life that are satisfying and those that warrant more attention.

For example, one's wheel might depict a high level of satisfaction in Work and Family, while showing a lower level of satisfaction in Leisure or Learning. This is fairly typical in younger families, where all energy is focused on economic survival and it never feels like there's enough time or resources for other pursuits.

In addition to the Wheel of Life, we also use another Money Quotient worksheet called the Financial Satisfaction Survey (see appendix). This survey directs clients to rate their current level of satisfaction in a variety of areas, such as their ability to save, their debt level, relationships with professionals and their comfort in talking about financial issues. This worksheet is a bellwether tool to help us understand and assess the areas of strongest comfort and/or concern.

We also collect quantitative data to help us grasp our clients' present situation. Among other things, you will need to have a very precise understanding of your clients' net worth, cash flow/budget information, taxes, retirement, education, career mobility, estate planning and risk management.

When collecting information from our clients, we are careful to ensure that we don't mix quantitative with qualitative data gathering. In our office, a junior planner often takes on the responsibility of collecting and crunching the numbers, while the life planners focus on the qualitative information. If you are a sole proprietor, you might consider asking for the quantitative information at a different time than when you are doing qualitative inquiry. In this way, you demonstrate that you see your client as a whole person, not just a list of numbers.

Looking Back:

As humans, we want to know "Why"; it provides a foundation for understanding our current behavior. Therefore, some of the most important issues to uncover, both for the planner and client, are the understanding of past money scripts—those messages we carry from childhood about money that impact our behaviors today. These money scripts tend to stay with us through our lifetime, typically without any level of awareness. To become aware of their money scripts, we ask our clients to address the following topics:

1. Lessons learned from each parent

2. Concerns as a youth regarding money

3. First experience with earning money

4. How money was used in the family (as a reward, for survival, to show control, to impress, as a way to reach goals, and so on)

5. Parental work ethic

6. One-sentence messages remembered regarding money

7. Money as a source of conflict in relationships

As a result of considering these topics, I learned a great deal about my own money scripts. My father grew up during the Depression and was not a spender. My mother, on the other hand, was eleven years younger and grew up with a totally different experience. Having lots of nice things was important to her. Their battles were fairly regular, and the mixed messages of "saving vs. spending" were a strong presence in my life. Since my mother was the more upbeat of the two, and my father more of a worrier, workaholic type, it seemed to me as a child that spending was way better than saving. Buying nice things was good, and worrying was bad. Therefore, I tended to be more like my mother in my habits. I may not have worried much, but there was definitely room for improvement in the way I handled my own finances and related to money. When I gained a greater awareness of my money scripts, I became more conscious and balanced.

What are your money scripts? Can you see how your past has affected your present? Is it possible that changing some of your attitudes or habits could impact your future success? I recommend that you take the time to look at your own patterns clearly. I also recommend George Kinder's book and workshop, *The Seven Stages of Money Maturity*. Understanding your own money scripts and their effects can benefit you on a personal level, while also making it easier for you to address your clients' money conflicts.

Recently, I met with a new client who came to me to talk about his impending retirement. It was an eye-opening experience that illustrates how money scripts, if unaddressed, can create significant financial and emotional stress. As extreme as this example may seem, it is not uncommon.

> *Dr. and Mrs. T sit in our conference room. In the Fit meeting, we'd learned that Dr. T had just received a buy-out from his medical practice and wanted to engage us to help create a financial plan for their future. My objective today is to assess the likelihood of success based on their past.*
>
> *As I enter the room, Dr. T is peering at a sheet of paper covered with numbers. Mrs. T sits with her arms folded tightly, looking positively negative. After introducing ourselves, Dr. T hands me the paper and states proudly, "Here's the buy-out from my medical practice! The numbers are staggering to me. I never imagined having $1.5 million in my hand at one time."*
>
> *"Of course you didn't," Mrs. T snaps. "You've spent every nickel that's ever hit your pocket and then some!"*

Dr. T's spine stiffens. It appears that he is about to shoot back when he instead sags further into his chair, throws up his hands in acquiescence and looks down at the floor.

"We owe the government, the credit card companies and you still buy everything in sight," Mrs. T continues. "The packages from your online purchases never stop, and now your career is over and we have nothing to show for it but this buy-out. After we pay off what we owe, there won't be much, if anything, left— and that's all we have in the world." She swivels in her chair to look at me. "Here, he's a physician and has earned tons of money and we have nothing to show for it. He keeps all of this hidden from me, I have no control; he doesn't listen to anything I say. I just don't know what to do!"

I listen calmly, waiting to ensure that she is done speaking. I can see that I will need to acknowledge the issues while redirecting their energies so this anger won't permeate our entire meeting.

"I hear the deep feelings that are involved here. And I believe that right now, it would not serve to continue the discussion this way. Therefore, in order to try and help you both, I'd like to start off with a few exercises that will help get a handle on what's going on, beyond the money. Let's start with an exercise called Money Memories [see appendix]. Please take some time to complete the twenty questions on the two pages in front of you."

I watch as they each begin answering the questions. After about fifteen minutes, they put down their pens. Dr. T looks confused. Mrs. T looks only slightly less miserable than she did before our meeting. Copies are made, and I pass back the originals to them. Dr. T looks down at his worksheet and puts his head in his hands.

"Dr. T," I begin gently, "how was that for you?"

He sits back in his chair, thinking. The room is very quiet while he seems to internally process what he's just written. Finally he looks up, his eyes glazed, and shakes his head. "I can't believe I've never realized this before today. Fifteen minutes ago, I couldn't understand what Amy was so upset about. How could I have been so blind?" He pauses and looks down at his hands, then picks up his worksheet. "It's all right here. My feelings of growing up without ... we were so poor; there was so much denial. Now here I am sixty years later, and I haven't learned a thing. All I've done is perpetuate the same cycle and put myself, and my wife, in precisely the opposite position I wish to be in."

I allow the words to sink in all around. "Those are some very powerful memories and even more powerful self-observations. It's probably going to take some time to really integrate and think about what you've realized here today."

I turn to Mrs. T, who has become very quiet. I scan her worksheet and ask if she wishes to comment.

"It's so interesting," she begins, her voice much gentler now. "My experience with money was so vastly different. Money was a tool for living. Although we didn't have very much, my parents taught us to save for a rainy day, to think through what was being spent, whether it was frivolous or important. I grew up respecting money, but nowhere near the experience that Jack had. It's so different!"

Dr. T, looks at his wife, listening intently. It is obvious that he is drawing distinctions between their experiences and the impact on their behavior. He shakes his head. "I've always thought of myself as having above-average intelligence. I am a very good physician, graduated top ten from my med school. But realizing that I have done nothing short of sabotaging my life, our life, because of these internal feelings ... well, I just feel plain stupid. How could I have never connected the dots?"

Tears begin to flow, unrestrained. His wife leans over and puts her hand on his. There are no words to be expressed. After a few minutes, the emotions subside. "Dr. T," I say gently, "was there ever a time when you felt in control of your money and in control of your spending?"

He looks at me for a good minute or two before answering. "Yes, Michael. When Amy and I were saving for our first house, we saved like crazy. I wasn't earning a lot; I had just finished my residency and Amy was paying the bills and watching the money. We did a great job together!"

His words hover in the air. His pride at their accomplishment seem to diminish as he realizes that since that time, when he has taken control over the money, things have gone straight downhill. He looks over to his wife. "I'm sorry."

Mrs. T sits quietly, lost in her own thoughts. I ask her if she would share her memories.

"Before we were married, I was very capable and handled my own financial affairs. I saved regularly, which was something I had learned from both of my parents. 'Work hard, save your money for your own security and buy things that are important!' they always said. I mean, it was okay to be frivolous every now and then, but the serious money was saved and invested, and I always felt secure. After nursing school, I shared an apartment with two other nurses, and I handled the finances for everyone. It was very nice and I managed to save a nice sum, before I met Jack."

"You are obviously very capable and focused," I say, smiling reassuringly. "It sounds as though your experience and attitude can help you both greatly in moving forward." I wait a moment, then continue. "OK, let's look at what's working and what needs to change and why."

Without missing a beat, Mrs. T says, "Clearly, we need to tighten our belts. We need to sell our house and see what's left after paying off the mortgage and line of credit. I think we will have enough left over to buy something small in Florida or

North Carolina. We need to get rid of our credit cards and make our spending footprint smaller."

I turn to Dr. T. "Any thoughts?"

Dr. T throws up his hands. "This is very difficult for me. I have a lot to think about. But clearly, big changes are necessary, and it looks like I need to turn the reins over to Amy in this area."

This is real progress. Still, I can see that both of them, especially Dr. T, are drained. They will need some time to process this experience before making any decisions about action steps. I look at them both, take a deep breath and say, "Mrs. T, Dr. T, we covered a great deal today, including some issues that are, to say the least, very sensitive and very personal. It took a great deal of courage to share some of these issues and challenges. Please understand, I am without judgment and have one item on my agenda, which is to help you improve your financial well-being as you move into the next phase of your life. It appears that there are some issues that you've just now started to deal with that would benefit from additional exploration and hopefully resolution. It is a process, but I believe you two have the strength and courage to see it through."

The stillness in the room is replaced by tentative assent from them both. Our meeting ends with their agreement to provide financial information to our junior planner and to complete two worksheets that will help them look into the future and begin to outline specific goals and financial musts. They promise to call our receptionist to set up our next meeting after the remaining worksheets are completed. Dr. T shakes my hand earnestly, then escorts his wife out the door.

Money scripts can be positive and affirming or negative and destructive. In the case of Dr. T, his messages came from a sense of lack, a Depression mentality that often results when someone feels deprived. His messages left him feeling badly about himself. In order for him to feel successful, he would spend money without consideration for the ramifications. It left him in a financial mess, and his relationship with his wife was at constant odds.

In our Life Planning practice, we have seen, without exception, that where money scripts have been dissimilar, there is greater conflict and challenge in reaching shared goals. Of course, this doesn't mean that widowed, single or divorced individuals do not face the same issues of broken scripts and behavior; far from it. However, dealing with one set of habits can be simpler than dealing with two dissimilar sets of behaviors and habits. These differences create greater challenges in establishing and working toward common goals—at least, until there is awareness, recognition, understanding and corrective actions taken. We have been most successful in helping clients when we've been able to:

1. Help the client see the impact of their past money scripts.

2. Look at times in their lives when they have been successful with money and help them recreate those conditions.

3. Ask the client to articulate what's working and what's not.

4. Create reasonable targets based on agreed upon action steps.

Once we achieve these tasks, we can look to the future.

Looking Forward:

The next part of the process is to help our clients look forward and really take hold of their dreams. When asking the client to look into the future, we are asking them to drill down to the essential core of their values and dreams. By connecting with their deepest values and dreams, they are able to articulate their financial musts.

In working with clients to create a future that aligns with their own unique dreams, we refer back to the Wheel of Life exercise. We show the client their Wheel of Life for the present and ask them to redraw it for their preferred future, a future that contains all the riches they value. We encourage people to dream big; at the same time, we also try to keep things realistic. As an advisor, you always want to strike the balance between motivating your clients and staying practical. There is an inherent tie between one's belief and one's ability to achieve, but it must be based on some level of reality. For example, even if I continue to work out at the gym every day, and hire the very best coaches and trainers, the probability of being signed by the New York Yankees as their star first baseman is still zero. Similarly, someone who was living in a state of financial crisis would not be dealing in a rational reality by visualizing the purchase of a 60-foot yacht within the near term. When a vision is real for the clients and is both viable and exciting, they are more willing, ready and, in fact, excited to make necessary changes.

The exercises direct the client to imagine various aspects of their life in the future, not unlike the exercise you went through in Chapter Eight. The client considers and writes what they value most, what their current riches are in each area of life, what action steps are appropriate to increase their level of satisfaction in each area, and what might be missing that could be added. In so doing, we help our clients visualize a future that is both practical and rich, both realistic and an expression of their dreams. We send these exercises home with the client and explain that they will require adequate time, focus and consideration. These are the exercises I gave to Dr. and Mrs. T at the end of our first data gathering meeting. The next time we met, it was as if a different couple had walked into my meeting room.

Dr. and Mrs. T look more relaxed than our previous meeting. There appears to have been a softening. It looks to me like Mrs. T is beginning to feel more control over their situation and is hopeful that they are now on a path to financial sanity. When asked about the visioning exercises I'd given them to complete, she sits up straight and the words come pouring out.

"There is an awful lot to consider here," she answers. "It was a bit overwhelming, at least at first. The first area that made me think is the relationship with my family. I have felt empty since the kids moved to North Carolina; I want to be close and accessible to my grandchildren and children. That is a must for me. Also, since Jack has some medical issues; I want to live in a place

where there are reliable medical services available. I imagined being in a community with nice and interesting people where there are learning opportunities and an active social scene, but nothing pretentious or pressure-filled. I've always wanted to take college-level classes, just for the fun of it. So, I'd like to be in a locale where there's a university or junior college or some sort of higher education options available. I am not overly concerned with my home, as long as it's comfortable and manageable; I don't want maintenance to be a full-time job. Mostly, I'd like a place where I can grow, explore and get out of this rat race. I just want to live a life that is full without being hectic, rich without costing a fortune and meaningful without the constant pressures of money!"

Dr. T nods as she speaks. "You've painted a very vivid picture of what's important to you. It truly came alive for me as you presented it," I say, then turn my attention to Dr. T.

"I am completely in agreement with Amy. I want a simple life, yet I need to be engaged. I am not a golfer and have certain limitations but am determined to begin a rational exercise routine. I would like to earn some income, and I would really like to do something with my hands, like working with models. I used to like doing that when I was a kid." He smiles shyly. "I would also like to write. It's been a secret desire of mine for a very long time. I have plenty of ideas."

"As long as they fit in our budget!" Mrs. T shoots out.

Dr. T, looking a little sheepish, responds, "Yes, yes, of course."

I smile at them both. "You've painted a pretty full canvas. While I cannot provide you with conclusions at this point, I now have an idea of what's important to you both, and we can begin to build the plan around those areas. I will have some follow-up questions, especially dealing with some of the specifics around where you wish to reside and the approximate costs to make a purchase." We cover a few more details; I answer some of their questions and then turn our conversation to a more complete description of their vision of life in retirement. Unlike the last meeting, we are now able to discuss specific action steps and how they will manifest them.

When clients are able to specifically identify their goals, dreams and needs, the conversation takes on new meaning. Clients then realize that you are building the plan around what they have identified as vital and critical. In order to get to this point, the advisor needs to clearly and specifically instruct clients that without their thoughtful consideration, the plan will not resonate with them, and the chance of success will be considerably lessened.

There are times, however, when clients are just not sure or are unable to imagine their future. This is especially true for people approaching retirement. This is when the advisor needs to ask specific questions to lead the client into considering the possibilities. For example, I had a client who didn't know when he would retire, as there was no age limit in his career. He'd never really thought about retiring, so he didn't know how his life would change if he slowed down or ceased working at some point. I asked him to consider possibilities rather than specifics, to weed out the definite Nos and build from the Maybes. Building a plan on Maybes is less impactful than a plan based on definites, but it can be helpful in moving one closer to finding the most comfortable and meaningful scenario. For example, I asked this client to imagine what his life might look like if he was to retire in five years and how that might change if he was to retire in ten. In his earlier scenario, he expected to be more active and engage in activities that might be more costly than if he were to wait for ten years, when his desires might be less extravagant. In each scenario, a different level of spending had to be factored into the plan.

Creating a vivid image of the future is one aspect of Looking Forward. It is the articulation of possibilities and is typically very broad in respect to life's possibilities. It has not yet been put through the "strainer" of financial or other realities. The next step is to begin to set goals that are realistic within the scope of one's resources and abilities. For Dr. and Mrs. T, this meant channeling their discretionary expenses toward lifestyle, learning and other activities rather than an expensive home. They asked me to help them put together a rational budget and both promised they would follow it. Simplicity and security, they had discovered, were key.

No matter how well we plan, though, life invariably has its surprises. As my grandmother used to say, "Man plans, and God laughs!" The only thing we know about unknowns is that they will occur, which means we can still plan for them.

When looking to the future, there are a significant number of variables that planners and clients must consider. Some are controllable, and some aren't. Such variables may be random occurrences, such as the effects of economic decline on a widespread basis, while other variables are dependent on client behavior. An appropriately designed financial plan will account for as many variables as possible.

Here are a few examples of variables that might affect the outcome of a plan:

1. Unanticipated Life Transitions

2. Health

3. Death

4. Disability

5. Long-term unemployment

6. Shifting or unclear goals

7. Unexpected inheritance

Many people do not consider the possibility of these variables, yet they must be taken into account when collecting data for a client's plan. I remember the response of one of my clients, a fifty-two-year-old woman, when I asked her how it would impact her life if her elderly mother became ill and needed support. She simply looked at me and said, "I cannot even begin to deal with that possibility." It took some time, but finally this client agreed to consider the possibility that her mother would require financial support at some point in the future. Thankfully, she reached this conclusion in time to factor these considerable costs into her financial plan.

Life transitions represent significant changes in our lives and the lives of our clients. In fact, one of the most important conversations we have with our clients is about life transitions, which can bring great joy or tremendous pain and typically have financial ramifications somewhere in the mix. We generally have the beginning of this discussion during our Fit meeting. The foundation for our discussion of life transitions is a Money Quotient tool called the Life Transition Survey (see appendix). This survey asks clients to consider a wide range of possibilities and whether they are currently experiencing these changes or expect to do so in the near term or the long-term. The Survey is broken down into the following categories:

1. Work Life Transitions

2. Financial Life Transitions

3. Family Life Transitions

4. Legacy Life Transitions

Some of the more difficult topics discussed might be: death of a spouse; aging parents; health issues; need for long-term or end-of-life care; and retirement or job loss. These conversations can cause a great deal of anxiety; however, the emotional cost of not having the conversation is of much greater consequence. For example, the shift into retirement holds many financial and emotional challenges. Perhaps for the first time in forty or more years, there's no office to go to and, for many, no more sense of purpose. This can be especially challenging for men, as they typically identify themselves with their careers. In the case of Dr. and Mrs. T, his shift into retirement meant not only a loss of income, but more importantly, a loss of his identity.

> *In the two weeks since our last meeting, Dr. and Mrs. T have been working on the Life Transition Survey, which they faxed over to my office in advance of our meeting today. I ask, "In your Life Transition Survey, you've pointed out several areas*

where transitions are imminent, such as retirement and debt concerns, and some others which are further out, such as 'Providing Long-Term Care for Self or Family Member.' Can you tell me more about your thoughts on these issues?"

Mrs. T looks long and hard at Dr. T, who is looking long and hard at the table. He takes a deep breath and looks up into my eyes. "Obviously, I am now facing retirement and all the issues surrounding that. Honestly, I think I have been in denial about this and other things. I see myself as a physician; it's all I've done for the last forty years, and now I am just a "Mr." It makes me wonder about my identity. I am used to the respect that comes with being a doctor, and now that's basically over. Who am I, and what do I do next?"

He looks so sad as he says this. There's nothing simple about facing the fact that what he has known most of his life is now gone. Instead of greeting each day assuredly, the rest of his life is now an entirely blank page. I want to empower him by reminding him of his own ideas and enthusiasm for what the future could hold.

"At our last meeting, you talked about your desire to write, to create, to build, to learn, to exercise, to spend time with your grandchildren and children. These all sound like exciting and meaningful pieces of a new life. You've worked very hard in your life, and now it is time for you and Amy to reinvent yourselves. It is normal to feel unease. That's why it is a transition—going from one phase to another. It's not only a change in income, but status, lifestyle and attitude. This transition requires a fresh mindset and thought pattern. It can be challenging." I let my words settle. "Any thoughts?"

Dr. T leans back in his chair and looks at his wife. "I suppose it will be a positive step to have our finances finally in line and to have a roadmap showing what we can spend without all of the pressure. He pauses, then smiles. "I guess I'll just have to learn to be a Mister."

"It's ok, Jack," I smile back. "I've been a Mister all my life, and it doesn't suck."

As you can see, data gathering entails being brave, being quiet, being specific, and being empathetic. Sometimes a little bit of humor can help, too. Each client situation will differ in terms of the time and persistence required for the investigation. It might be relatively straightforward or incredibly complex. Your job, as an advisor, is to ascertain as quickly as possible the knowledge you will need to understand your clients well enough to create a plan that represents their resources, values, dreams and goals and to ensure that their habits promote actions necessary to achieving success.

The next step is the integration of the qualitative information you've gathered with the quantitative data to produce a plan that is unique to your clients' needs. Before you turn the page, take some time to think about your process and whether you effectively understand your clients from the perspective of their past, present and future. Are you devoting adequate time to the issues beyond the numbers? If so, turn the page. Let's put it all together!

Chapter Eleven

Bringing the Plan to Life

"The general who wins the battle makes many calculations in his temple before the battle is fought. The general who loses makes but few calculations beforehand."

~ Sun Tzu

Let's face it. Any financial planner who's been in the business more than a minute can obtain financial information and enter the data into a computer program. In fact, I'd go so far as to say that it doesn't even take a financial planner to fill out a data input form and plug numbers into boxes. What the skilled financial planner does is marry the data to a context. Question: Can a client get from here to there based solely on the numbers? For many financial planners, especially those with a particular leaning towards the "quant-side," this is the essential question. The solutions provided by a quant-based planner might come in the form of cash flow commentary, net worth projections, estimated retirement distribution, college-planning needs, new portfolio composition, risk management proposals, tax-oriented ideas or estate planning suggestions. The basics: all good … but not good enough.

As Financial Life Planners, our job is to provide our clients with a richer, more meaningful experience that evolves into an intimate understanding of their values, dreams and goals. In order to bring their plan to life, we must completely understand their financial musts and build the plan around the issues, transitions, challenges, hopes and dreams that will help our clients live a balanced, integrated and more satisfying existence. It is this deep understanding of the inside data that allows the Life Planner to integrate the hard numbers and create a plan that best represents the client. I select life-planning exercises based on the needs of each individual (see appendix for the worksheets listed below). Typically, the exercises I use during the fit meeting and data gathering are:

1. Financial Satisfaction Survey

2. Wheel of Life

3. Money Memories

4. Life Transition Survey

5. Visualize Your Future

I have a copy of each exercise in my files, along with my notes and observations from our meetings. The notes synthesize what I see, hear and glean from the conversations that follow each exercise. These notes are vital to my understanding the client, their behavior, their expectations, their experiences and their desire to adopt a life plan that reflects their true values, goals and dreams.

There are no templates that translate these exercises into a course of action. That is where the art of planning comes into play—understanding the nuances of what is being said and what you observe. Is there a connection or disconnection between words and actions? For example, one client completed a *Financial Satisfaction Survey* and showed fairly high levels of satisfaction in many areas. *The Wheel of Life* also demonstrated a good balance in most components of their life, especially in terms of their financial life. Yet, when I examined their financial information, I found significant levels of debt, inaccurate recordkeeping and a lack of understanding of many basic financial concepts. When reviewing their *Money Memories,* it became apparent that this client grew up seeing that money was used to impress.

Money wasn't talked about unless it was a source of conflict. Given those factors, it was no surprise that there was a disconnect between this client's words and reality. This conflict had to be addressed in order for the plan to be successful.

Bringing the plan to life is the art and science of marrying the qualitative and quantitative information. The planner must hear, understand, synthesize, translate and communicate the information into a cogent, workable and realistic step-by-step plan. There also needs to be a clear understanding of the human factors that can mitigate, support or destroy the chances for the clients' success. Some of those factors are:

1. Client Behavior

2. Financial Education

3. Time and Attention Devoted to One's Financial Life

4. Motivation

Client Behavior:

We can develop a plan that is perfect; we can hit all the elements of great planning, point out all the strengths and weaknesses, make recommendations that will play like a Stradivarius violin. Where the whole thing breaks down is in our clients' behavior, often affected by money scripts and peer pressure. What can you do to increase the success ratio? Richard S. Kahler, CFP®, President of Kahler Financial Group in South Dakota, a recognized industry leader, advisor and author, described it to me this way: "Today's Financial Life Planner must hone and nurture the skill of understanding client behavior. It's an essential survival skill for any true financial planner and their practice." As usual, the first step is acknowledging what you don't know and gaining that information.

I recommend that you begin with several books that might help gain further insight about the importance and challenges of client behavior, such as *Wired for Wealth* by Rick Kahler, CFP® and Drs. Ted and Brad Klontz; *Drive: The Surprising Truth About What Motivates Us* by Daniel H. Pink;

Your Money and Your Brain by Jason Zweig; and *Nudge* by Richard H. Thaler and Cass R. Sunstein. Another essential tool is a series of worksheets created by Money Quotient, including the *Financial History, Money Memories* and *Personal Insights about Money*. These tools are essential in helping the planner and client understand some of the factors that lead to certain behaviors.

Financial Education:

There is a knowledge gap in our country, a wide chasm between what we know and what we need to know in order to make good financial decisions. Why is this so? Generally there are three major reasons: we don't teach it in our schools, we didn't learn from our parents and we have little time or interest beyond the mundane and necessary tasks of bill paying or data collection for income tax preparation. In my experience, very few clients come in with a reasonable amount of information or knowledge about financial issues. This is a lose-lose situation.

It is in all parties' best interest to expand your clients' knowledge base. We believe that where knowledge doesn't exist, we need to help fill in the gaps by providing resource materials, discussions and articles that will increase comfort with some of these topics. Sir Francis Bacon said, "Knowledge itself is power." Our objective is to empower our clients. Depending on the level of knowledge, I recommend several books for our clients such as *The Wall Street Journal Complete Personal Finance Guidebook* by Jeff Opdyke; and *Ernst & Young's Personal Financial Planning Guide* by Ernst & Young.

Time and Attention Devoted to One's Financial Life:

Do you remember the exercise from Chapter Four on Self Inquiry with the blank circle? We will frequently ask our clients to complete the same exercise, a pictorial representation of how they spend their time. The pie chart shows how they spend their time on a percentage basis, showing their work time, family time, leisure time, community time and time devoted to their financial life. Would you be shocked to know that the financial slice is hardly noticeable in the grand scheme of their lives? This exercise has been helpful for our clients to see when they are not investing enough time in their own success. We also frequently recommend clients engage in the following activities:

1. Use a computer program (like Quicken) to capture their spending by category.

2. Reconcile their accounts monthly.

3. Review expenses monthly, looking for extraordinary items.

4. Actively contribute to a savings and/or investment program.

5. Consider which financial issues are imminent and how that impacts their financial plan.

6. Think forward: what do next month, next quarter and next year look like? Any anticipated changes? Identify what financial issues are on the horizon (short, mid- and long-term).

7. Devote time to discuss current financial issues with their partners.

8. Talk about money with their children; bring them into the conversation.

9. Write down questions to be relayed to us for discussion or clarification.

It is generally clear who handles the bulk of the financial matters in a household; there's typically one member who carries the ball and the other spouse is either tangentially involved or not at all. This might be because of disinterest, lack of understanding, time or fear. One party might feel incapable and allows the other to do it all. I have seen this countless times, especially when dealing with divorcees or widows who might never have been involved with the handling of finances. The level of fear is palpable, but with support, knowledge and experience, their comfort and confidence increase incrementally over time.

Experience has demonstrated that when one person is not involved in financial decision-making, there is a real possibility that if goals are not met, or there's a problem, the reaction will be blame, anger and a sense of victimization. The fix here is to understand why one party is not involved and what it will take to bring them into the process. You want all parties to feel competent and empowered, regardless of who is taking the lead role. Addressing the issues in a direct, open and honest method is helpful in moving to a more balanced level of participation.

Motivation:

I will talk more about motivation in the chapter on Monitoring the Plan; however, in any aspect of life, the proper amount of motivation and support are vital in making changes. There has to be a very good reason to go through the pain and process of changing habits. When it is real and important enough, change happens. Without that motivation, the plan's chances of success are limited, at best. The key is small, incremental, meaningful steps that give your client the taste of successes. Each small success becomes the bedrock on which to build the next success.

Now that you have all the relevant information, it's time to bring the plan to life. While this step is obvious to many, it may help to see one method of marrying the financial and life-planning data. Here is a process that works well for us:

1. Accumulate and review all Life Planning exercises.

2. Accumulate and review all meeting notes.

3. Review Financial Data with Junior Planner.

4. Junior Planner creates basic output from software.

5. Senior planner uses information from Steps 1 and 2 to provide guidance for Junior Planner.

6. Senior planner reviews output and creates additional scenarios as necessary.

7. Senior planner reviews plan and considers how it will be impacted by client behavior, financial education, time and attention to financial matters, and motivation.

8. Senior planner creates list of action items needed to implement plan.

9. Senior planner creates planning memo of action items.

As you review the list above, consider how this differs from a traditional planning approach. Certainly, steps 1 and 7 are unique to the Life Planning process.

Once the plan is built, synthesized, processed and tested, the planner must communicate with the client in an effective and specific manner. Handing a client a sixty-page financial plan is not effective. You might even say it's slightly sadistic (unless your client is an engineer, architect or actuary, in which case make it eighty pages!). To keep things clear and simple for our clients, we typically create either a planning memorandum or letter that enumerates the goals, findings and necessary action steps.

The Planning Memorandum is the synthesis of the financial plan, providing a step-by-step guide to help move the clients from inaction to action or from inefficient action to a more efficient mode of operation. The key is to begin with the items most important to our clients, this way obtaining greater enthusiasm and buy-in. When preparing this communication, be sure to keep in mind how your client processes information. The more overwhelmed the client gets with this kind of information, the more simply we word the memo. Please note: I do not mean that the information is dumbed-down. It's just presented in terms that are explicit, clear and free of any confusing terminology. Sometimes, it is helpful to create a flowchart, graph or mind map to display how the details fit in with the overall picture in the memorandum. Here are some examples of plans brought to life:

> *Reviewing the notes and data from our meetings with Joan and Pete, it is clear that their major focus right now was gearing up for retirement. The future care and support of Joan's mother is also a concern, especially since the timing of this will probably coincide with their second child beginning college. They want to feel comfortable that they can handle all these transitions and implement a better, more focused ac-*

cumulation plan. They also need to improve their financial education beyond balancing their checkbook each month, so they will feel more comfortable with the long-term decisions that are on the horizon. These are the main goals that covered the majority of our discussions together, so we focus our thinking and planning around these questions: Will they have enough to support their lifestyle? How will their life change after retirement, and what are the financial ramifications of those changes?

The next step is to examine the financial information compiled by Jim, our junior planner who handled their quant-based data gathering. Here's what we find:

1. They received a substantial tax refund for the past three years—both federal and state.

2. Recordkeeping had been haphazard.

3. Their homeowner's, auto and medical insurance had very low deductibles.

4. They had positive cash flow each month that accumulated in their checking account.

5. College funding through 529 plans for their eldest son's college tuition was sufficient, but the plan for their daughter, a sophomore in high school, was funded to about 30% of the projected need.

6. Pete has maxed out his 401(k) contributions.

7. Joan has not maxed out her SEP.

8. Their discretionary costs are about equal to their fixed costs.

9. They are paying for a medical plan at their son's college, but he is still covered by their current plan.

10. *Pete's 401(k) allocation is mostly in cash, as he didn't know how to invest the funds, and his stockbroker offered no assistance.*

11. *Joan's SEP Plan is invested in sector securities of mutual funds.*

12. *Their risk tolerance is moderate 60/40 Equities/Fixed income.*

13. *They expect that within the next three years they will need approximately $15,000 per year for Joan's mother's support.*

14. *Pete expects a 4% salary increase and a bonus of $50,000 ($30,000 after taxes) annually.*

In preparing Joan and Pete's plan, we see an abundance of opportunities to help them close the gap of satisfaction. Here is their Planning Memo:

> *The purpose of this Planning Memorandum is to outline and synthesize the financial data gathered in discussions, exercises and observations from our meetings. It is broken down into Foundational Steps, Strategic Steps and Future Actions. I recommend that you read the memorandum before digging into the analysis in the attached Financial Plan. The essence of the memo is to highlight your areas of concern and help you achieve your goals, dreams and financial musts. The Financial Plan contains your net worth, cash flow, future projections and other analysis specific to your goals.*

The Next Step: Preparing for Success

Foundational Steps:

1. *Financial Education*

   You have both stated your current discomfort with basic financial knowledge. We believe, as you begin to consider transitioning into the next phase of your life, it is vital that you gain sufficient competency to be comfortable with financial issues. We recommend the following:

a. *Attend a basic financial management course at local university (see attachment).*

b. *We will provide you with a copy of* The Wall Street Journal Complete Personal Finance Guidebook *to help provide greater comfort with financial topics and concepts.*

c. *We will extend an invitation to our next "Basic Estate Planning" roundtable luncheon, which we hold quarterly in our office. This meeting will enable you to increase your knowledge of estate planning topics as well as meet other clients who are experiencing similar life transitions.*

d. *We recommend that you both devote a predetermined amount of time each month to review, analyze and discuss your current financial position. This typically can be done in less than one hour per month. The desired outcome is to become more familiar with your spending choices and their impact on your overall strategy and ability to make financial choices.*

Strategic Steps:

These strategic steps are meant to refocus your thinking and actions to help you achieve your goals. Your priority and desire to be able to retire within a reasonable time-frame, educate your children and help support Joan's mother for the foreseeable future will require some minor shifts and changes.

1. *You are cash flow positive each month, but the surplus is not strategically saved or invested. We believe that by setting up an automatic transfer each month to cover a variety of your goals, including short-term needs, college funding, retirement and support considerations, you*

should work more efficiently in meeting your goals, needs and dreams.

2. *It is evident from your tax returns that you are consistently over-withholding taxes, both federal and state. A better use of these funds is to alter your withholding to meet your projected tax liability for a break-even. According to our estimates, you should be able to realize approximately $800 per month in available cash. These funds need to be accumulated directly towards your specified goals as outlined in your financial plan.*

3. *We have noted that your homeowner's, auto and medical insurances are all at the lowest deductible possible. We believe it is prudent to increase the deductibles to $2,500 for each policy. We expect this to save you approximately $3,000-4,000 per year. These funds need to be accumulated directly towards your specified goals, as outlined in your financial plan.*

4. *We have further noted that the medical insurance taken for your son at college is a duplication of coverage. Eliminating this coverage will save you $1,200 per year.*

5. *We have noted that your discretionary expenses are substantial. Based on your plan, we recommend a rollback by 8%, which will help fund college and support Joan's mother.*

6. *According to your risk profile, your portfolios, both nonqualified and qualified (401(k), SEP, etc.) are inappropriately allocated. We believe an overall structure of 60% Diversified Equities to 40% Short term Fixed Income is better aligned with your risk tolerance and the expected return needed to help accomplish your goals. We have provided specific recommendations in the text of the plan.*

7. *We believe that in order to meet your goals, Joan needs to maximize her SEP contributions annually.*

8. *In order to meet the college funding needs, the amount specified in the Educational Cost analysis should be invested monthly in your daughter's 529 College Savings Plan.*

Future Actions:

1. *Creating a retirement lifestyle is a challenge for most people. We recommend that you devote time to considering which activities, passions and interests you might wish to explore.*

2. *We will provide several exercises in future meetings to help you focus on post-retirement life.*

3. *Future planning meetings will be specifically targeted towards exploring various planning scenarios.*

In reviewing the above memo, can you pick out which items would be quant-based and which required qualitative data gathering? Can you see how the deep understanding of Joan and Pete's situation became the bedrock of the financial plan? If not, go back and review the list again; pencil in your thoughts about each item. Again, the goal of working with clients is to understand them well enough to create a workable plan that is understandable and presents changes that are reasonable and reflect the clients' burning desire to achieve a specific set of goals. What could be more important than giving your client the gift of being heard, understood and presenting them with something to be truly excited about?

Dr. and Mrs. T represented a challenge because they were dealing with a track record of ineffective behaviors and a lack of success. The challenge would be to help them feel successful and empowered to make good decisions that support their dreams and goals within a controlled spending environment. This is definitely a crawl/walk/run; they are initially going to require a high degree of monitoring and handholding. Our planning memo confronts their most critical issues of mutual accountability and the need for goal-setting and careful implementation:

Planning Memorandum

You are emerging into a new life stage. Congratulations! Change is all around you, in your lifestyle, geography and even your ideas about life, money and what is truly important to you both. In order to guide you safely into your new life, we need to approach these changes with a degree of excitement and enthusiasm but also with great care and intention. It is necessary to work together, communicate and make incremental changes. This planning memorandum is not intended to be complete, but only to handle the initial stages of your transition. Once we have successfully achieved this segment, we will present the rest of the plan.

The First Step: Preparing for Success

Financial Accountability:

As you know, the success of your Financial Life Plan is dependent on working together within a rational financial framework. You have agreed that in order to live your retirement dreams, there needs to be greater transparency and commonality of goals and actions. Therefore, within the constraints of your current financial universe, we recommend the following:

1. *All financial decisions are made jointly within the framework of the budget designed during our work together.*

2. *Each party works together to capture financial data (Quicken, MSN Money, etc.) each week, making sure that each expenditure is properly categorized and accounted for.*

3. *You will use only a debit card for your normal purchases and a credit card only if the funds have been pre-allocated for the assigned cost.*

4. *A liquid reserve of savings/money market funds are kept at a level that provides you with six months of expenses.*

5. *You will send us your monthly expenditures report within ten days of the close of the month for our review.*

6. *We will meet every two months by telephone and face-to-face three times during the year.*

7. *The assets remaining after the sale of your residence and settlement of all outstanding debts will be allocated according to the analysis in your plan. The goal will be to create a steady stream of cash flow, while allowing for a level of growth for the long-term.*

8. *You will continue to search for part-time income opportunities that fit within your comfort level. We spoke about the possibility of working at the Walk-in Center on a fill-in basis. This income would provide the funds necessary to allow for greater personal exploration within your stated desires and goals.*

9. *It is understood that since this is a new phase of life, that you approach it with a "learner's mind," without judgment or conclusion. Pre-planning activities, involvement and opportunities should be fun, interesting and meet your needs and desires. This process typically will require trial and error and an open mind. HAVE FUN!*

As with Joan and Pete's planning memo, can you find the different aspects here which are more qualitative in nature? Notice how understanding your client as completely as possible provides you with the advantage to speaking to your clients' values, goals and dreams.

In one sense, "Bringing the Plan to Life" is an ending, but in another, it is the beginning. The data has been gathered; the information, both quantitative and qualitative, has been gleaned, analyzed and synthesized into a workable roadmap to help your clients move from thought to action. The heavy lifting is done! Now it is time to present the plan to your clients and prepare for their reactions. As always, your objective is to stimulate their imagination and enthusiasm to make whatever changes are necessary to live their dreams.

Chapter Twelve
Presenting the Plan

"All you need is the plan, the road map, and the courage to press on to your destination."

~ Earl Nightingale

Before I incorporated Life Planning into my financial planning process, the presentation of the plan was something of a hit or miss. One particular instance comes to mind.

I'd been working with Mr. and Mrs. Glenn for a few months, collecting all the numbers and talking a bit about their financial goals. Most of all, I knew that they wanted to retire at the age of sixty-five; this became the cornerstone of their plan. I crunched all the numbers and drew up a plan that would allow them to retire at sixty-five. Hallelujah! Filled with excitement, I called them in for a meeting to present their plan. Not five minutes into my presentation, however, and Mr. Glenn was flipping through the book-sized plan I had given him, muttering to himself. When I asked him what he was looking for, he said, "The beach house."

My left eyebrow rose. That was my only response for several seconds. Beach house? Who said anything about a beach house?

Mrs. Glenn looked at me suspiciously. "After we retire, we want to be able to travel, of course, and buy a house. A nice big house, big enough for all the kids to come for family gatherings. Preferably on a beach. We've been thinking about this for many years. Perhaps we didn't make that clear …"

Right. They certainly hadn't made that clear. In fact, this was the first time I had heard anything about it. But whose fault was that? Mine. It was my responsibility to get *all* the pertinent information from them before creating the plan. Now that this very large piece of the puzzle came into play, the plan I had so meticulously prepared was basically worthless. Sure, they could retire at sixty-five, but no way could they afford extensive travel or a real estate investment. Back to the drawing board.

By the end of the meeting, everyone had a bad taste in their mouth. They were frustrated because there had been all these meetings and all this build up to presenting a plan that didn't include all of their desires and objectives. I was frustrated because now I was going to have to redo the plan, costing me a lot of extra time and energy, and I'd probably lose them as clients anyway. Even after I drew up a plan that better reflected their needs, some weeks later, the damage was done. I never heard from them again, and I don't blame them.

Has anything like this ever happened to you? Did you ever stop to wonder why? Perhaps you didn't gain enough of your clients' trust for them to share information with you, or you didn't hear it. Maybe you didn't have the methodology to take what they were saying and implement it into their plan. Maybe you were caught in the middle between wanting to get all their information and being afraid of being too invasive or being a pest. It's very common for planners to have that fear, thinking, "I don't want to ask them that; it's a difficult question and hard for me to ask." Without looking like the Keystone Cops of financial planning, it is true that many planners trip over themselves in their efforts not to be too intrusive or a pain in the neck or ask questions that might make clients uncomfortable. By applying Financial Life Planning techniques, you can feel comfortable asking the important questions. It's part of the process that your client expects to go through. Since introducing Financial Life Planning to my clients, they now expect me to get straight to the point and announce the elephant in the room. Not only is this normal—it's welcome, and my clients are grateful that someone cares enough to ask the difficult questions from an earnest desire to help. Not to judge, just to help.

If you've done your work correctly throughout this process, constantly getting feedback from the client, the presentation step is a no-brainer. It is merely a summary of what you've been doing all along through the discovery and discussion process. The total meeting time is generally twenty to fifty minutes; it's a good idea to keep it short. There shouldn't be any surprises at the presentation.

There can be plenty of surprises, however, when you don't go through this process. Unless you provide time for the client to quantify and articulate their goals in the context of their past, present and future, there is no way to prepare a plan that reflects their financial musts and realities. They might have talked about wanting to retire, but did I understand what a retirement lifestyle meant to them and how they would practically be able to achieve it? Even when I did get it right, there was less chance that the clients would implement the changes I'd suggested. They were not clear about their own goals, so they were less willing to make the necessary sacrifices to attain these goals. By implementing life-planning exercises in the process, I ensured that the presentation of the plan would be both the easiest and most exciting meeting of them all.

Preparing the Ground:

In many ways, the presentation of the plan is the same as all other meetings you will have with your clients. Like all other meetings, you prepare yourself and your clients before jumping into the big stuff. I liken this to tilling the soil before planting seeds. You make the ground more receptive for its upcoming evolution. Ensure that the room is ready. Take the time to prepare yourself mentally and emotionally for the meeting, reviewing any notes and taking some quiet time as needed, so you can bring your A-game. While this meeting is often exciting and simple, you never know what your clients will bring with them when they walk in the door. You can be on top of the world but they may have just received some bad news or may not be feeling well. At any rate, you need to be on your toes and ready to meet them at their level, as always.

As in all other meetings, start off by asking for their hot burning questions. The questions may have nothing to do with the topic of the meeting, and that's okay. Some questions need to be answered immediately to put the client at ease. Otherwise, I will address questions at the end of the meeting if they are unrelated to the plan presentation itself. By this time, they expect you to ask for their HBQs. If you don't ask, this very well might add a feeling of doubt as something has unexpectedly changed.

After addressing their questions, refer to the individual action summary sheet to check in about any open items. At this stage in the process there generally aren't any open items; most of them will have been addressed during the data gathering process. However, it is important to maintain the momentum you set from the very first meeting. By addressing the to-do list, you once again demonstrate that you are on top of the process and expect them to be as well.

Before jumping into the plan itself, I always take a few moments to articulate my understanding of the client's financial musts. This may sound obvious and repetitive, and it is—that's why it's so important. By validating your client's musts, you again show that they have been heard. There is no gap between what they've said and what you've heard and therefore, the client has it firmly in their mind that the plan you're about to present is built around their top needs and musts.

Once you've repeated their top goals, ask them how important it is for them to live their dreams. Yes, you've talked about this before. Talk about it again now so they are more willing to make the changes necessary to achieve their goals. They understand that these changes are necessary, and they get excited and motivated to do what is necessary. This is all about motivation. Even if they are motivated today, they may not feel the same way a few weeks from now when it comes time to actually make changes. You can expect that there is going to be some pushback at certain times—they aren't feeling it or they go back to old habits. This is why I do so much reinforcing, every step of the way. Prochaska's model of change posits that before a change is complete, there comes the step of maintenance and support. You remind them and reinforce in every meeting that you will be there to support them through the entire process. This is the time when you need to be a cheerleader.

Even with simple changes, it's somewhat inevitable that your clients will hit the wall at some point. They will reach for the cheeseburger, and it's your job to say, Okay—make it a mini, and go back to eating healthy tomorrow. Every single step of the process, remind them that this is about living *their* values, living *their* dreams, therefore change is necessary, and change is an incremental process. In this way, when they feel resistant, they will know that this is what you were talking about and that you are there for them. Instead of getting disheartened and giving in to the resistance, they can pick up the phone and give you a call. Your clients need to know that there will be challenges and that you are there to support them. You don't just crunch numbers, give them a printout and send them on their way. They need to hear this over and over again.

So you ask them yet again, What are you willing to do to make this happen? This question helps clients understand that making substantive changes in their habits are necessary. Maybe they will need to create different processes for themselves, change some habits, or cut back some discretionary expenses. If you will be suggesting that they make any change, large or small, in their habits, processes or beliefs, you will ask this question to prepare them yet again for the fact that change is a process.

With these steps, the ground is prepared. The seeds are planted; it's time to inspect the harvest.

Presenting the Plan and Planning Memo:

Without further ado, it is time to hand over the goods. I first present clients with the planning memo, give them time to look at it, and ask if they have any questions. Before moving forward, be sure to answer all their questions. Most importantly, I want them to digest the fact that the planning memo says: *If you follow these carefully outlined steps, your chances of living your dreams are greatly enhanced.*

What about the plan itself? The plan document is a rather ominous book. It contains the analysis of their current financial condition, along with scenarios that would encompass the changes we recommend. It can be quite intimidating for a client to tackle this document without guidance. It is easy to become overwhelmed. When I present the plan with the planning memo, I explain that we won't go through it page by page but that it contains the numbers to back up what we've suggested in the memo. If there is something specific in the plan I want them to see, I'll lead them there directly. At the meeting itself, I do not want them to have to digest all that data, and we will have already gone through all the numbers at previous meetings. We focus on the conclusions, action steps and necessary behavior changes; they can go back to the plan to find the back-up data that supports our conclusions if they wish. The key is to begin with the items most important to our clients in order to keep them enthusiastic and willing to invest in the recommended decisions and changes. Still, if they have questions or the desire to review all the numbers, we certainly will.

Take as much time as they need. They might want clarification of an assumptive number based on an index average or inflation, but generally they don't have or want to know all the details. Out of a hundred plans, probably about two people go back and look at the numbers in a detailed manner. If they are more analytical, I may go through a spreadsheet or two, but I typically don't spend more than a few minutes on it. I want them to keep their eye on the ball, focus on the fact that with these changes, they can realize their dreams. I want to leave them feeling really good and knowing they can move closer to their dreams, not worrying about three hundred pages of charts and graphs. I will invite them to go through it at home as they desire and encourage them to take their time with it and come up with questions for our next meeting. At this point, I want them thinking about how successful they can be, not feeling exhausted and like they don't know what the hell just happened. When they come out feeling powerful and energized, we are on our way.

While presenting the plan, I don't recommend spending too much time talking about implementation. Depending on their personality and issues, I may give clients a few things to implement that are simple and don't require much time—for example, having their accountant do a tax projection or calling their insurance agent to change their deductible. Larger issues and money management issues will wait for the implementation meeting, when I will lead them through a process to better ensure understanding and motivation.

Still, not all plans are filled with great news. Some clients will need to make drastic and immediate changes that may be a challenge for them. The point is, they won't be hearing that for the first time at this meeting. They won't schlep all the way to our office to hear that their plan failed, and they'll have to work till they're one hundred years old and eat cat food until that time. Any dejection about having to face significant challenges would come earlier. I can't think of any situation where a client left a presentation meeting feeling like, This sucks and you suck and I'm outta here! That's never happened.

Before Life Planning, however, that kind of dejection was much more likely. We would have to say things like: Your plan failed and it looks like you won't be able to do x, y and z. Because of the Financial Life Planning process, however, this meeting is reaffirming and helps the client feel more complete and focused. In this way, you can continue to keep the client motivated even while admitting that the road ahead may not be easy.

What are the benchmarks of a successful presentation meeting? Your client walks out feeling heard, understood and that you've translated all your work together into a feasible co-created solution. They feel confident that throughout the implementation and monitoring process, you will continue to be there with them every step of the way. How can you accomplish this result every time you present a plan? It's all in the preparation. Make sure you go into that meeting mentally prepared, feeling confident, strong, aware and knowledgeable. All of your documentation is in perfect alignment. You feel successful and ready. Your energy level is positive and strong but controlled.

I truly believe that a lot of the success of the meeting depends on your own mental attitude going into the meeting. If you walk in not at the top of your game, unenthusiastic or not being fully present, the meeting will suffer and the outcome will be weak. The plan could be great, but if you demonstrate a lack of positive energy, the success of the meeting will fall flat. It will reflect wherever you are.

In addition, if you haven't prepared well, haven't listened well, haven't heard your clients, then the presentation meeting will be a disaster. You won't have happy clients; in fact, you won't have many clients at all. If you've done your job properly from the beginning, this should be your easiest meeting with the fewest number of challenges, because it's just a reiteration of what you've discussed all along: why they're there, what they care about, and how to get it. As Shakespeare said, The past is prologue.

While most of your clients will be upbeat about this meeting and its results, they won't all react the same way. It would be a mistake to go in with the expectation that all of your clients will be doing cartwheels and ready to get things rolling. As with any meeting, they could be having an off-day or dealing with a crisis at work or an issue at home. If you come in prepared to give them a high-energy spiel and they're not feeling it because of something in their life, and you're not paying attention to where they are in the moment, you will fall short of providing what they need. You always want to go in emotionally neutral and not overpower your clients. Read what they need. You can read their level of enthusiasm and excitement. Just by walking in the door, you're typically going to know how they're doing by looking at their faces. You'll know when you're hitting the target. You can just feel it! There's a flow to what you do. There's a flow to the conversation. The meeting goes by in the blink of an eye. You feel like you just won Olympic Gold. That's when you know you've hit the bull's-eye. It's like an athlete being in the zone.

> When I walked into the meeting room to present the plan to Joan and Pete, I could literally feel their excitement in the air. They were sitting there sipping green tea, as usual, but there was also a palpable feeling of positive energy and expectation in the room. We greeted each other with hugs and handshakes and it seemed to me that they could hardly wait to get started. Their vast smiles were a vast shift from the uncomfortable wariness of our first few meetings.

> "Good morning, you guys! How are you?"

> "We are so excited for this meeting today, Michael," Joan says. "After all we've put into this, we're really looking forward to seeing what you've developed around our concerns and goals. This has truly been a wonderful and affirming process!"

"Thank you, I am very gratified to hear that you have enjoyed the process. I know it can be laborious at times and sometimes stressful. However, we have always kept your values in mind in all our meetings, which is energizing and has produced positive results. Let's begin as we always do before we get into the heart of the meeting. Any Hot Burning Questions?"

They look at each other and shake their heads.

"Let's begin. During the course of our time together, you have continued to verbalize and write about several items that are very important to your definition of comfort and success. Those items are your desire and need for greater financial education so that you are more comfortable in making decisions. You also articulated the importance of providing funding for your daughter's college education and supporting Joan's mother within the next several years. Also vital to your concerns is the ability to live a comfortable retirement in which you have no fear of outliving your assets. Does this sum up the essence of our conversations and your financial musts?"

I watch as they mull this over. After a few moments, Joan nods her head. "Yes. Those are the things that are most important to us. Those are the things that if accomplished would make us feel very comfortable and successful. Right, Pete?"

"Exactly," Pete proclaims. "After all these years of work and struggle and ups and downs, we need to be able to put our heads on the pillow at night without worry. Accomplishing those items is exactly what we need. Thank you!"

Joan looks at me pensively. "Michael, what's the verdict? Can we accomplish these goals? Can we do these things?"

I pause before answering—not to build suspense, but to acknowledge how meaningful this question is to them both. "I have heard your excitement and your wishes, and now we are *at the threshold of a new and exciting chapter. My question is: What are you willing to do to make this happen?"*

"Are you saying that we need to make significant changes in order to accomplish these things?" Joan asks. "Michael, we are committed to this process. We don't expect you to tell us that we need to do anything drastic like sell our house or get a second job. I don't think we'll have any problem following your suggestions. Right, Pete?"

"Of course! So what's the deal? Is this major surgery?" Pete asks.

I can't help but smile. "Joan, Pete, you have worked diligently and have been open and thoughtful in your responses. The reality is, you are well on your way to making your dreams a reality. The changes we have isolated are relatively small changes. Many of our recommendations are clean-up items and efficiencies. Some will take a bit of decision-making on your part. Let's go through the Planning Memo, which is a synthesis of our recommendations. Next, we'll look at aspects of your financial plan so you can see how we came to these conclusions and what the ramifications of following this plan will look like."

I hand copies of the memo to Joan and Pete and ask that they take a few moments to read the document. As they read, I watch them carefully, looking for reactions, both positive and negative. I see enthusiasm and relief as they take a few minutes to look over the memo.

"Michael, there is nothing here that presents a problem or even a major challenge. I am particularly excited about the list of financial courses and workshops that you've prepared for Joan and me to consider. Most of the other suggestions are just creative and informed steps to helping us achieve our goals," Pete says happily.

Joan nods her head in agreement. "You also mentioned a plan with more details."

"Yes, here it is. As I said before, the planning memorandum is the synthesis of the financial plan. Here is a copy of your complete plan." I hand a copy of the financial plan to each of them. Their eyebrows shoot up and they look at each other with consternation. "It's a lot, I know! I don't expect you to digest this now, but we will go through two basic scenarios so you see the possible impact of the changes we are recommending. Let's turn to tab #1, Base Plan. This first page shows your current net worth and a projection, based on the assumptions that we've discussed. You can see those assumptions under that tab in the back of the plan document. We've projected out to your life expectancy and ascertained—here's the good news—that the success of the plan is likely! However, with too many variables, it could become tenuous. Do you see that?"

Joan and Pete scan the page. I wait until they both nod their heads.

"Great. Let's now turn to Tab #2, Scenario #1. This page shows the possible outcome with the changes recommended in the planning memorandum. Do you see the change in possible outcomes?"

Again, they nod.

"Behind this initial page of both tabs are the Cash Flow projections and other analyses relating to college funding, portfolio allocations, risk management, tax projections, retirement distribution analysis and some legacy issues that we've discussed. There is a lot for you to review and digest, and I recommend that you take this home and look through it, taking the time you need to assimilate the information and come back with any questions. Of course, you can call me if you have questions, and we'll get together for our implementation meeting after you've had time to review these documents. Do you have any idea at this point how much time you'd like to allot to review this information?" I don't want to push them or put any pressure on

them, just get an idea of our timeline, get our next meeting on the calendar and kept the momentum going.

Joan and Pete talk dates for a moment. They decide to look at it over the weekend and set up a meeting for next week, unless they find questions that need additional clarification. "We don't expect to have any major questions since this all sounds like what we've been talking about all along, but just in case," Pete says.

"Great. I'll note that in the individual action summary."

"Michael, I agree that we need time to read all this and understand the fine points and some of the other concepts; rest assured we will tear into this quickly. I am so excited to make these changes and to devote the time necessary to attend some of these financial workshops and courses. I see that as pivotal in the long-term for our comfort. In the short term, most, if not all of your suggestions look like no-brainers." Joan looks at her husband. "In fact, I'm not sure why we didn't make some of these changes a while ago, especially with our son's health insurance policy. I am most excited about the way you have suggested setting up gathering the surpluses we create by implementing the changes you've highlighted. That will help us immeasurably!"

"I feel the same way. The other thing that frankly surprises me about this plan is the simplicity. I expected a lot of mumbo jumbo and painful cuts and obtuse investment schemes. Instead, you have made it very clear and easy for us to move closer to living our dreams. I am grateful for that," Pete says.

It feels so great to hear him say that. It's an amazing feeling to know that the people you are working with feel great, feel like you've heard them and that you've synthesized their dreams and helped them set a proper course. It's so emotionally powerful. It's a truly wonderful feeling. The only thing better is seeing the results of their work. When you lead people into an A-ha! moment, you know: I made a difference today. I did something good. I led them to a place that is meaningful to them. Those emotional responses are one of the reasons that I do what I do. "I am gratified by your reactions," I say.

"After you've had a chance to review the memorandum and plan in greater detail, we will set a meeting to begin implementation. The implementation plan will include a step-by-step to-do list to effectuate the changes most important to you. We'll discuss this in the next meeting, but for now I want to call your attention to a few items that will involve other professionals. You will need to contact your CPA to advise you on withholding changes. Since you will be assisting your mother, Joan, I suggest you speak with an Elder Care attorney to make sure these transactions are structured appropriately. They are relatively easy things to check off. You will find that the quicker you check things off the list, the more power and momentum you will have in moving your plan forward. No need to contact these people until after our implementation meeting; I just wanted to give you a heads-up now. Any questions?"

Joan and Pete leave the meeting all smiles and excitement. Perhaps for the first time when dealing with their finances, they feel empowered and in control. Most importantly, they saw the reflection of their values, hopes and dreams mapped out on paper, in a step-by-step approach.

Wouldn't it be great if all plans could meet the immediate and long-term needs of clients? Often, unfortunately, that is not the case. Joan and Pete had their finances essentially in order, but many clients don't. In such cases, you may have to encourage the client to cut back or delay some of the things they're hoping to do. Providing motivation is more important than ever. There will undoubtedly be disappointment but by talking openly about regret, you can help them work past it to create satisfaction around the newly created and more realistic goals. The best way I've found to do this is to center the conversation on core values. I ask questions, such as: What is most important in your life? What brings you joy and satisfaction? What scenario would allow you to put your head on the pillow at night? By maintaining focus on the positives and feelings of satisfaction, thought patterns shift away from disappointment and feelings of inadequacy.

This brings to mind a story of a couple that came to me with significant financial problems. Their concerns were not about how to buy the beach house, but how to survive. They were unable to meet their current obligations and were slowly being strangled by credit card debt. In creating their financial plan, I kept in mind the essence of their concern: how to live within their means without fear of insolvency. They needed to break some life long habits and beliefs that kept them living patterns of behavior that sabotaged their ability to live comfortably. Our conversations centered on questions like, How will you feel when these struggles are behind you? What will it look like to live within your means? How will that feel? What images are created when you are living without this debt hanging over your head?

The key is to present these questions appreciatively. I've been fortunate enough to work personally with Edward Jacobson, PhD., who is a coach and author of *Appreciative Moment,* and I have incorporated Appreciative Inquiry techniques into my work with clients. This methodology is especially helpful in working with clients who have experienced challenges and might have negative inclinations about their abilities to succeed. I recommend it highly. Another resource advisors might look for is Jacqueline Kelm's book, *Appreciative Living: The Principles of Appreciative Inquiry in Personal Life.*

By utilizing imaging and feeling questions, we have been able to build a bridge to a level of commitment and even excitement regarding the steps necessary to get clients solvent and out of debt. Can you see how these types of questions can be helpful, if not essential, in helping clients through tough choices? Again, it is the client who is creating his or her own success, based on their willingness to make changes that are in alignment with their core values.

> *Dr. and Mrs. T's path from conflict to resolution was a difficult one. For them it was chaotic, both personally and financially. They were forced to confront the facts that they were not among*

the affluent. They would not enjoy the comfort of financial ease as expected of a "successful" physician. The paradigms had to be shifted. They had to wrestle with several big issues. Dr. T felt entitled to spend without consequence, while Mrs. T was living in crisis mode from not having a solid or secure financial or personal life. Marriage counseling played a big role in their newly rediscovered ability to communicate effectively. Our work together helped them focus on a life that was realistically within their means and centered on their core values. Without doing all this work before the presentation meeting, I would have expected a total meltdown. Instead, we were able to find common ground.

"Good afternoon, you two. Do you have any hot burning questions you'd like to put on the table before we start?"

"Michael, this experience has brought so much insight for both of us," Mrs. T begins earnestly. "We are anxious to bring this to the next level and create some tangible movement so we can see how all the pieces of the puzzle fit. Is that what we're going to accomplish today?"

"Yes, exactly. Our objective today is to review the strategies we've developed that will satisfy your shared vision. I know I've said this a hundred times, but your shared vision, as you've articulated, is to live the next phase of your life without financial worry. Your core values center around living without financial pressure and to explore life in many aspects, and you are willing to live within the scope of a reasonable budget plan. You also said that the community in which you plan to live has a university nearby where you can attend classes at nominal costs. This is very important to you both. In addition, since your daughter and grandchildren live close to your new home, you expect to engage with them a large part of your life, especially the grandchildren. Is that right?"

"Yes," Dr. T says, "our new community has so much to offer, culturally, academically and with sports and other physical

activities. We expect that our transition will be rather smooth. The question is, can we do it?"

"The good news is: Yes, you can do it, if you follow a disciplined plan very carefully. Here is a copy of your plan for each of you; the planning memo is on the first two pages of the document. Please take a few minutes to read the planning memorandum and then we'll talk about your plan and the success steps involved."

With that, Dr. and Mrs. T dig into the planning memo. The only sound in the room is the turning of pages and I can see that they are fully engaged. After several minutes, they stop reading. Dr. T looks at me with a wan smile on his face. "In this scenario, it appears that you will continue to provide us with a great deal of support as we ease our way into our new phase of life. You have asked us to keep you very fully informed about our progress. I am battling with two different feelings; one, I am extremely grateful that you are so committed to our success. On the other hand, I feel entirely incompetent that I require this amount of handholding. Does that make sense?"

"I hear your concern," I answer. "Allow me to frame this a little differently, please. Let's use the example of learning a new skill, say, tennis; I know you enjoy that sport. Well, think of being new to the game. Perhaps the first thing you do is hire a coach and begin to take lessons twice a week. Your coach will make suggestions about what equipment you need, your swing, your arm angle, your footwork, your approach to the game— everything necessary to increase your skills from beginner to the next level up. Eventually, you are a competent player, and perhaps you wind up taking lessons periodically rather than twice a week. Your confidence level increases as your game improves. Make sense? Well, this is the same idea. We are directing you, coaching you, guiding you, with the expectation that with the confidence of your abilities to handle this new lifestyle and financial position, you will no longer require our close monitor-

ing and frequent assistance. It will eventually become a periodic update and review. Does this help?"

Dr. T nods. "I guess it makes sense when you put it that way."

Mrs. T has been quiet throughout our conversation. When we first met, she had been so frustrated by their lack of communications about financial matters that it manifested as anger and aggressiveness in our meetings together. Today, she reaches out to her husband and puts her hand on his.

"Michael, for the first time, I believe we can live a comfortable life financially. I believe we are, for the first time in a long, long time, on the same page about what we truly care about. We want to spend time with our children and grandchildren; we want to explore, learn, create and enjoy ourselves without worrying about where the funds will come from to pay our taxes or wondering if the practice will throw off enough of a bonus to help us catch up with our credit card debt. We are so grateful to you and your team. We finally have a true track to run on and are set up to communicate effectively on financial decisions. This has been life-changing."

Wow, did that feel good to hear. "I am extremely gratified by your statement, Mrs. T."

"Oh Michael, please call me Amy!"

"Amy, I am confident that together, once you have read through the plan and see how it integrates your needs, wants and life goals, you will find that it falls into place very well. It is a significant life transition on many levels, so you will need patience and discipline to make it all work. You can count on the fact that things rarely go as expected, so we have tried to build in as much flexibility for changes necessary. I believe that if you follow the steps outline, 1–9, we will work through whatever we need to.

"Now, let's talk a little about the future, beyond this first step. Once we have established a routine that works, we will be able to expand on the planning scenarios. For example, if you are able to create some income, we might have even greater ability to check off more items from your wish list. It depends on many factors, but let's keep first things first. Let's get you situated, debt-free, cash flow comfortable and established in your new community. How does that sound?"

Dr. T looks me in the eye. "We're ready!"

Presenting the plan is another opportunity to articulate your clients' values, dreams and goals. It is the time to reset, restate and reinforce the reason why they engaged you to begin with. This is a time where you must be prepared mentally and emotionally to listen and watch carefully for reactions. You have laid out the steps necessary to get from here to there, based on your clients' statements, discussions, Life Planning exercises and hard data. You have taken all the quantitative and qualitative information and created a plan of action. Your job is to be energetic, enthusiastic and sensitive to what your clients are experiencing. This is one of the most exciting meetings in that you now have the opportunity to deliver something that the client has waited for since the fit meeting. Enjoy the experience.

Chapter Thirteen

Where the Rubber Meets the Road: Implementing the Financial Life Plan

"We must become the change we want to see in the world."

~ Mahatma Gandhi

It's time. After all your tinkering and testing, it's time to open up the garage and take the plan for a ride.

At the last meeting, you unveiled the plan and discussed the planning memo with your clients. Soon, you will be meeting again to discuss implementation. It's their job now to review the plan and prepare their questions. What about you? Basically, your work is already done. Before the implementation meeting, you need only review their planning memo and consider which recommendations are the most important now. If you have done your job properly, your planning memo will indicate which are the highest priorities. You will have already created a strategy for addressing these priorities in the short and long-term; your task now is to consider how best to present the strategy to your clients. There's not much I can say about this in a book. It's an intuitive process that will be different with every client. You may gauge that one client is ready for a lot of major overhauls, while another needs to move more gingerly. This is where your understanding of their history and their past successes can give you an indication of how they will proceed.

Implementing the plan is a step-by-step approach of taking something theoretical and creating a specific action. Therefore, the goal of the implementation meeting is to fix responsibilities, timelines and specific steps to completion. As in past meetings, you will take some action points, and your clients will take others. Some actions might require the work of a CPA, attorney or other specialist. As we've discussed, it can be difficult for people to embrace change, yet your clients' success, and therefore your own, often depends on changes being made. The key to effectuating change is what I call KTR.

K: Keep the steps small and simple.

T: Time matters.

R: Make it REAL.

KEEP the steps small and simple! This allows the client to add it to into the mix of their daily activities without it consuming their lives. Changes need to be manageable and cause as little friction as possible. For example, I had one client who wanted to undertake financial education. I'd recommended various classes, but he just couldn't find a way to attend them without giving up things that were more important to him. We agreed that he should forgo the classes and read a book or two instead. Another way of keeping things simple is by clarifying who will do what. It may sound obvious, but how many times have you heard someone say, "I thought you were going to do that?" It's a lot easier to create a workable system up front by using a form such as the Individual Action Summary (see appendix).

TIME Matters. It always does! It is vital that there is a fixed time for completion. Open-ended assignments lose momentum very quickly and feel overwhelming. Therefore, we ask our clients to affix a time period to any specific act, whether it is as simple as going online to reallocate their 401(k) or meeting with an attorney to redo their estate documents.

Accomplishments need to be measurable so that checking them off the list is a pleasure, rather than a pain.

Make it **REAL!** In order for a client to take action, it must be demonstrated that it will improve their lives. So the acid test is to ask this question before asking a client to undertake anything: Will this action bring you closer or farther away from your stated goals and dreams? If it brings them closer, fantastic! If it doesn't, why do it?

By transforming thought to action in this manner—assigning responsibility, setting timelines and getting a buy-in—you will watch your clients take on the implementation of their plan with confidence and a feeling of success. No matter how large or small the action, you want them to feel successful every step of the way.

Once you have the plan and action steps figured out, you might assume the implementation meeting will be a no-brainer; you've already presented the plan, and all you're doing now is walking them through the action steps. Right? Well, any planner who's been around more than a week knows that expectations like this can and will kick you in the teeth and leave you by the side of the road from time to time. Different issues become sticky at different times. Priorities and realities shift. I had one client who told me at our implementation meeting that she wanted to bring her daughter, an MBA, into the planning process to help her better understand the decisions she'd be making. We kept the meeting very brief and rescheduled for a time when her daughter could join us. Another client had taken on a new job between our two meetings so we had to reconfigure some of his data before moving forward. Therefore, at the implementation meeting, as in all meetings, be prepared for anything.

A typical Implementation Meeting Agenda might look like this:

1. HBQs

2. Review Plan Summary

3. Answer Clarifying Questions

4. Reorder Priorities, if necessary

5. Create To-do's

6. Set timeline and accountability

7. Set next meeting

Let's see an implementation meeting in action.

> *Dr. and Mrs. T look tired. They are acting pleasant enough, but I can tell it would be best to keep this meeting short. After covering the preliminaries, I get right to business.*
>
> *"Dr. and Mrs. T, one of the first steps on the implementation plan is to get your current house sold. Tell me, are you planning on selling it yourself of through a realtor?"*
>
> *"Definitely through a realtor. We wouldn't know the first thing about it!" exclaims Mrs. T.*
>
> *"Do you know anyone with whom you'd feel comfortable working?"*
>
> *"Yes," answers Dr. T. "Our neighbor Jane is a realtor and we trust her. It's her street, too, and I am sure she'd want to put a great family next door and get the best price—after all, it's her property values as well. Who could be better motivated?"*
>
> *"Not to mention that as a friend, she told us she would cut her commission," adds Mrs. T.*
>
> *"Excellent! Who is going to call her and get the ball moving, and by when? I need a firm date for this action step."*
>
> *"I'll call her tomorrow." Mrs. T says. "She's told us that we can do all the required paperwork within a day or two, so let's write down that the listing will be done by Thursday."*
>
> *"Fantastic! The next item on the memo is to understand the tax liability both past and present. While we do have an idea, it is best to firm it up clearly. Who will call the accountant and by when?"*

"I already have a call into her based on the planning memo," says Dr. T. "She's away until Monday, so I expect, giving her a few days to find her desk, that I will hear from her by Wednesday. It shouldn't take more than two weeks to assemble the required information. So let's say, by the fifteenth of the month."

"That's great! Moving right along: The next item is rolling out your pension and 401(k) from the practice to your IRA. While we prepare the paperwork to establish an IRA, you will need to contact your benefits administrator for the forms necessary to effectuate the rollover. When will you do this, Dr. T?"

"Well, the effective date of the buy-out and separation is the eighth of the month. I was told I can contact them anytime after the eighth. So, I will call on the ninth and begin that process. How long does it typically take to get the funds transferred?"

"The process can take anywhere from two to eight weeks, in my experience, depending on the custodian. The paperwork will require Mrs. T to sign and have the documents notarized, so there are steps involved. If you submit clean paperwork, it typically goes more smoothly. However, any little glitch can kick it out of the system and cause substantial delays."

"Would you or your staff review the paperwork for us before we submit it?" Dr. T asks.

"Of course; that is normal for us to do, as well as enter the new trustee's information and your account number. I will add that to our Action Summary. When do you think you will have the paperwork to us? This way, I can put a time stamp on it."

"I will pick up the paperwork on the ninth and complete as much as possible. Then we'll go get it notarized, probably at the bank or maybe at our attorney's office. I should have it to you no later than the eleventh."

"That's fine. It will take us a day or two to complete and review, so we will submit the paperwork directly to your TPA and send you a copy of the documents by the fifteenth."

"Wow," Mrs. T says, her eyes wide. "A lot of things are being accomplished in a rather short period of time, but strangely, it doesn't feel overwhelming. I feel like we're really moving forward. If all goes as planned, by the fifteenth of the month our house will be listed, the tax information gathered and transfer papers for the pension and 401(k) will be in process. This is GREAT!"

I'm so happy to hear this. They even look less tired than they did a few minutes ago. There's a lot more to discuss, but I don't want to push it. Dr. and Mrs. T have a lot of dramatic changes to make in the next year or so. Instead of taking on too much right away and getting bogged down, I want them to walk out of here feeling as refreshed and confident as they do right now. They will need all their confidence and motivation in the months ahead.

"Well guys, we've gone through approximately one-third of the planning memo. Rather than continuing, we will stop here and reassess your progress in thirty days. If we have crossed off these items as agreed today, we will continue down the implementation list to the next grouping. It would be counterproductive to add more to your 'to-do's' right now. Besides, these first steps must be accomplished before we tackle more; one step builds on the next. For example, it doesn't make much sense to begin getting serious about your next home until your house is listed and we have a feel for the market. You are not going to carry two properties; therefore, we need to go just so far down the path before we can continue. Does this make sense to you?"

"Yes, completely! While there's a part of me that wants to keep going, I know it would soon become overwhelming, and the focus would diminish. It looks like you've laid out a sensible and rational construct for implementing the stages of our plan so that we can begin the next phase of our life with strength and *confidence. Having said that, though, I guess I should ask if you see potential problems in what we're attempting?"*

"That's a great question, Amy. Even while taking care of these steps, you must also remain vigilant about your expenses. As we discussed in our last meeting, in order for this plan to be a success, you must maintain your cash flow management very carefully, making sure your discretionary outflow is within the prescribed limits. With so much in motion right now, this is an extremely critical time. As you well know, it's easy to just let things go, and we cannot afford that at all. Meanwhile, we'll be keeping an eye on the housing market and how this may affect the selling price of your home and therefore what kind of new residence you'll be able to afford. Please continue to consider the option of renting in case you find nothing that falls into your range to buy.

"I also want to acknowledge that this is a time of significant transition for you both. Between selling your home, looking to move, retiring from practice and changing spending habits, there's a lot going on! I hope that even as you are vigilant with these action items that you will also remember to be gentle with yourselves and acknowledge that there's a good bit of emotion attached."

Dr. T smiles wryly. "Yes, Amy has our therapist's phone number on speed dial! No, really, she's been a great help, and we've agreed to see her periodically as we go through this whole experience."

"That's great to hear, Dr. T. Rest assured that we will remain focused on the positives here, such as successfully accomplishing your action items."

Dr. and Mrs. T look at each other and nod their heads. We are off and running.

Chapter Fourteen

Monitoring and Completion

"Perseverance is not a long race; it is many short races one after another."

~ Walter Elliott

We are nearing the end of the book, but the process of change is just beginning. Think of a big change you've made in your life. Look back at the timeline between your decision to change and the time when you could honestly say the change was complete. Can you track the process? We're talking about big stuff here; changing any habit, let alone longstanding financial habits, is big stuff. Shifting patterns can at times feel like a Sisyphean nightmare. But when given the right amount of motivation, support and a clear vision of the end goal, success can be yours!

Once your clients begin implementing their plan, they move into the final stage in Prochaska's model of change: Maintenance. For some people, this stage may be the easiest and shortest. For others, this is where the work really begins. One way or the other, once your clients enter the maintenance phase, they still need you. In fact, they may need you more than ever. It's up to you now to monitor the plan and how it is being enacted. Prochaska calls this phase Maintenance, explaining that with careful monitoring, new habits become firmly placed and change is established. The monitoring he speaks of can be broken down into three steps: *rein-*

forcement management (encouragement), *helping relationships* (support) and *stimulus control* (motivation).[16] You will provide all three.

The ability to achieve permanent change will vary from client to client and depends on many circumstances, for example, the magnitude of the change, the client's attitude and motivation, along with the amount of encouragement and support needed to make the change permanent. In the presentation and implementation meetings, we openly discuss the degree of change necessary and the degree of difficulty it might entail. These conversations help establish the number of follow-up meetings, phone calls or other communications necessary to check in and monitor progress.

As with the implementation step, the way you monitor your clients' plans will be different for every client. Your goal is to provide the right amount of encouragement, support, and motivation—at the right time. You may need to meet more often at the beginning—or later in the process if you notice things are beginning to slip. At each monitoring meeting, you must reassess your clients' current standing in light of the changes still to be made. As with all meetings, you may need to shift your plans if clients come to you with new information or are more or less willing to act on your recommendations. Like your clients, you too must be willing to make changes to the plan if necessary.

In the best case scenario, the life-planning process will have been so effective that your clients will be extremely self-motivated in acting upon their plans. They will see that their positive actions are indeed making their dreams come true and your monitoring meetings will be a series of celebrations. Using Joan and Pete as an example, there were small refinements to be made but no radical changes necessary. They were both business people and were motivated to make necessary alterations to achieve their goals. After defining the necessary steps in our presentation meeting, we set up time defaults—the time when the last step was to be completed. We then set a meeting at the outside parameter of the time default, which in their case was six weeks. The purpose of that meeting was to see what was completed, how well things were working, and what unexpected issues arose as a result of the changes.

Working with Joan and Pete was a pleasure, although not particularly challenging. We needed to see their accumulations increase, and if they didn't hit the expected numbers, we would need to understand why. All in all, they wouldn't need a great deal of monitoring to ensure that our recommendations were implemented. We were, in essence, the cherry on top of an already voluptuous sundae. They were eager to see the progress and would readily call if they ran into any roadblocks. We decided to meet semi-annually with the option to add meetings if necessary.

Our first semi-annual meeting was basically a check-off meeting, noting what was accomplished and what was still open. Almost all items were completed and most importantly, Joan and Pete were able to see the effect of the changes on their accumulated income. We showed them how those changes had an impact in the short run and reflected directly on their long-term success. Joan and Pete were energized by the results and opted to engage in more life-planning exercises to help them look ahead and create a clear vision and plan for the next stages of life.

Unfortunately, not all client experiences are quite so tidy. With some clients, in order to achieve success, profound change is necessary. The law of physics speaks very clearly here: for every action there is an equal and opposite reaction. For planners, that means that for every change you recommend, you can expect to experience commensurate pushback, regret, fear and lack of consistency. You can best help these clients by persevering with your practice of KTR: *Keeping the steps small and simple; setting timelines;* and *making the need for change realistic and real.*

As in every meeting, the success of your meeting rides on communication skills. Knowing what to say and when is an art form and takes resolve and practice. It demands sensitivity to what is being communicated verbally and nonverbally. It takes commitment and patience on your part to ease your clients back on track. I have found no better method than beginning with the positives and trying to change the focus from negative to positive. No matter how dire the situation, begin by putting your clients' successes in front of them for them to see, thereby enlisting the aid of their eyes as well as their ears. This kind of reinforcement is very powerful. Writing their words down and leaving them up where they can be seen provides clients with a constant reminder of their achievements. This kind of motivation can provide the focus needed to deal with the negative issues.

Please note that the purpose is not to deny or shroud the negative issues. Those problems remain and will be dealt with, but first, lift the client's vision beyond the immediacy of pain to something more satisfying. Beginning with the positives makes the rest of the conversation more approachable, more open and much more productive. Knowing that you can see possibilities—even when they cannot—opens your clients' minds and gives them hope.

Showing appreciation for success is a cornerstone of our practice. Never was this more important than in the case of Dr. and Mrs. T. They left our implementation meeting feeling enthusiastic and confident about the road ahead. We met a few more times over the next couple months to discuss ongoing implementation steps and so I could monitor their progress. They managed to sell their house and moved into a rented villa in a retirement community in North Carolina. At every meeting, I saw that other critical action points were not being completed. After the move, they couldn't commit to future meetings in person, so we agreed to meet on the phone every few months. Years of destructive habits, mistrust and pain lay on the road behind them. They were excited about living a new life, in a new location, with a new outlook; but change is not always that easy. One day, about six months after our last face-to-face meeting, Mrs. T called. She wanted to set up a face-to-face meeting. They were making the trip North just to see me. Though I hoped otherwise, the phone call did not necessarily bode well.

Dr. and Mrs. T walk into the conference room looking more like they had in our first meeting than they did in our last: he like the kid with his hand in the cookie jar, and she fit to burst.

"Good afternoon! I'm happy to see you and am glad you found it important enough to come up for this meeting." I begin.

I hardly get the words out before Mrs. T says, "Oh, Michael, this is too important to leave to a phone call. It's been six months since we met last and I must tell you, things are a bit, um, unsettled."

Given the concern on their faces, I'm guessing this is something of a euphemism. "Tell me more."

Mrs. T looks sharply at her husband. He takes a deep breath. "Our budget is, uhhh, not quite working out as we'd hoped." He looks nervously at Mrs. T.

"Not as we hoped? I'll say! It seems as if we are bleeding money. With the moving costs, the furnishings and some of the things we've needed to get settled, it's been a tidal wave and it feels as though we are spending without any control."

There is so much anxiety in the air. I pause a few moments to make sure they've said all they need to say and allow the energy to settle a bit.

"You two have experienced some very major transitions in the last year. Tell me, what's working well? What do you feel good about?"

Their silence matches mine as they look at each other with surprise. It's probably been a while since they looked at the positives.

"Well," Mrs. T begins slowly, "it's wonderful being so close to our grandchildren and children. We're lucky in that we have really nice neighbors and have begun to make some very nice close relationships. Hmm ... oh yes, there's a community college right down the street with a very wide course selection. And the classes are very inexpensive, with a special rate for seniors!"

"That sounds great! It sounds like your family life, community and learning areas are beginning to fill out nicely, just as you wanted. How about you, Dr. T? What's good in your world?"

"Well, as Amy said, it's great to be close to the kids. And yes, the neighbors are quite congenial. I was contacted by several pediatric practices looking for an on-call fill-in, which is exciting,

but I am still waiting for my paperwork from the State Board to allow me to practice. That is so frustrating. I just don't know what is taking them so damn long! Still, I feel good, physically. I go the gym daily and we walk each evening; it's a new feeling to be active, and I am enjoying it."

I write down the positives on the white board as they speak. The mood in the room shifts a little bit, becoming more relaxed even as Dr. T expresses his frustration about the delay with the State Board. I take my time, allowing their comments to marinate a bit in their minds and hearts.

"It certainly seems there is a lot to be grateful for at this point."

Mrs. T shrugs. Dr. T almost smiles.

"Before we discuss your challenges, let's reframe the goals. I will read what you communicated in our meetings. If anything has changed, please let me know. OK?"

They nod.

"You told me that your dreams consisted of living near your children and grandchildren, living in a community that was welcoming, having opportunities to grow intellectually, be physically active and lead a full and productive life with financial comfort. Does that sum things up fairly well?"

"Yes, for the most part," admits Mrs. T. "But even with all the good stuff, we are still really stuck on the financial comfort piece. It is feeling very, very tight and uncomfortable. The bills keep coming in faster than the income."

"Your plan included that you would both work together in making financial decisions, and that you would work together in handling the checkbook. How is that working?"

The silence is deafening. They both shift uncomfortably in their seats, and Mrs. T's jaw tightens.

"I suppose from the reaction that it's not working too well. Tell me more."

Mrs. T shoots Dr. T a look that says, "Time to pay the piper!" With great effort, he looks up from the table. "I guess it's harder to change habits that I imagined."

This is a moment of truth. I'm not letting anyone off the hook, so I remain silent. Eventually Dr. T continues.

"Well, I guess you could say that my spending on things has, uh, not curtailed as much as I had planned. With Amy being involved with the grandchildren, I guess I haven't done too well communicating, and now the credit card bills have become, uh, well, larger than I, I mean, we are comfortable with. I am feeling rather terrible about this, as if I am digging us into another hole."

Mrs. T's face is getting redder and redder. She takes a deep breath, and I can see that she is trying very hard to control her anger. "Let's be honest here. He says he 'guesses' he's not doing well with communicating. Michael, I don't even know the balance on the credit cards. He's kept it from me and told me to wait until this meeting to discuss it!"

This really is the moment of truth. I pause another moment before asking, "Well, what is the balance on the cards?"

Sheepishly, he pulls out a folder. "The Visa is a little over $13,000 and the Mastercard is under $5,000. So, $18,000 give or take."

Mrs. T's face is going from red to purple. It looks like she isn't sure if she wants to punch him or just cry. I jump in before she explodes.

"Dr. T, it appears that your issues surrounding money are really deep. I would like to propose a ten-minute recess to give me time to think about what you've told me. If you would like some coffee or tea, Ashley would be happy to bring some in."

Shooting from the hip is never a good idea. Take the time necessary to allow everyone to thoughtfully consider and decide on the next step. Sometimes the best decision is to close the meeting, and sometimes it is better to move forward. In the case of Dr. and Mrs. T, they had traveled to New Jersey from North Carolina, so sending them home would hardly be a productive step. I needed a few minutes to digest the situation, consider what I had heard and focus on solutions. My delivery was as important as my content. My demeanor needed to be tough, yet not judgmental. If I excused the behavior and the problem, it would just keep happening. It was time for non-emotional truth. I took several deep breaths and allowed my mind to settle itself.

The room is silent when I reenter. Both of their eyes are squarely on me. They are ready. So am I.

"Dr. T, as a physician, you know better than anyone that you can diagnose and prescribe treatment. It is up to the patient to follow directions. It appears in this case that the patient is unwilling to take his medicine. I have a comment and a recommendation. My comment is that unless you address and deal with this issue, your financial life will be a disaster, and your dreams and goals will certainly crumble. My recommendation is to seek out some help. I suggest that you contact Rick Kahler and Ted Klontz, who have devised a program called "The Healing Money Issues Workshop." This might be just what you need to deal with your inability to curb your spending and live more responsibly. Ashley will provide you with the contact information on your way out.

"Amy, you need to take control of the checkbook, as we discussed, and Dr. T, you need to surrender your credit cards. I will consider how best to deal with the debt after I see your updated numbers. I would like to receive it no later than next Friday. In addition, Dr. T, I would like you to contact the State Board to see the progress of your paperwork and to perhaps elicit the help of the doctors who've offered to make calls on your behalf. I think it is time to channel your attention to creating capital

rather than spending it. Your plan did not have a lot of leeway, and your guarantee to make changes has not materialized. I realize it is a problem, but now I need your commitment to seek out a real and lasting resolution. Any questions?"

Dr. and Mrs. T sit still. As they absorb the words, their faces soften. Mrs. T no longer looks so angry. Perhaps she realizes that she, too, has dropped the ball. Dr. T actually looks a bit relieved. It's not easy to keep such an ugly secret, and I think he is more than ready to refocus.

"OK, Michael, I hear you loud and clear," Dr. T says, putting his hands up in the air. "I will call the doctors and do the other things you suggest. I'll even give Amy the credit cards. But I have to admit, I don't like it. The change feels really big."

"Yes, Dr. T, it is big, so let's break it down into steps. What do you think might be your best first step?"

Mrs. T chimed in, "Well, other than me taking control of the finances, REALLY this time, I suppose going back to look at the budget that we created and seeing where things stand."

"Exactly! What's after that?"

"Looking at our fixed expenses?"

"Yes, keep going."

"After the fixed costs are paid, see how much is left in our discretionary bucket."

"And?"

"Put 10% of income away into our emergency fund goal. Michael, did we destroy the chances of living our dreams?" Mrs. T asks nervously.

"No, your chances are not destroyed. Delayed, maybe. I want you both to know that your dreams are possible, but the process

of change must be deliberate, meaningful and permanent. I want to add one more piece of the puzzle as a way of helping you get on track. We need to meet more often, so I can better monitor how things are going. At the end of each month, I'd like you to email me your monthly expenses and then we need to have a conference call the following week to do a check-in. Let's see if greater contact will help keep you on target. I have to tell you that unless you make the necessary changes, I do not see a favorable outcome for achieving your goals. I think, at this point, we are teetering on some very dangerous ground. There will not be many more chances to turn the ship around. Any questions?"

They shake their heads. I hope that now they are crystal clear that the success of their life plan is dependent on their making real changes. There is nothing more to say.

I have heard mainstream planners call Financial Life Planning "touchy-feely." Really? What's touchy-feely about telling someone that they are staring down the barrel of a loaded gun? The fact is, our job is to announce the elephant in the room, to speak honestly and openly, without judgment and without anger or even ownership of the outcome. Being an effective Financial Life Planner is like being the perfect mattress: not too soft and not too hard. Frankly, there is a certain amount of intuitiveness in knowing which to be and when. A successful planner has developed an instinct that is borne of experience and the openness and comfort that comes from knowing your client. Monitoring the plan requires sufficient knowledge of your client and their needs along with their personalities, strengths and weaknesses.

The key is creating a relationship of interdependency. The client and planner must work in concert to create a methodology that produces the desired results. Interdependency in the client-planner relationship requires that each party is working towards the same goal. My objective is to have happy, successful clients who become my raving fans! In order to make them fans and promoters of my firm, they need to experience at every level—from our first meeting on—that they are valued, considered, heard and understood. My drive to bring them the greatest experience requires that our focus be on their success. That means providing whatever level of support, encouragement and assistance is possible. It also requires honesty, frankness and knowing what the client needs at a given time.

Monitoring the plan includes a series of ongoing steps that keep the implementation moving forward. Keep the focus and attention on whatever is going on in the client's life that might affect the success of their stated goals and dreams. Monitoring requires vigilance to pay attention to whether stated goals and dreams have changed and how the plan may need to adjust accordingly. Typically, following plan implementation, we will meet with clients several times during the first year to check in and make sure things are going according to expectation and what, if anything, has changed in their lives and thinking. Depending on the client, we will look to do a plan update every year or two. This gives us a quantitative view of success in a more structured format. Clients need to know that they are heard and understood, and they also want to see the numbers that back it up.

Have you ever witnessed someone realizing their dream? Have you witnessed someone facing up to a challenge—taking ownership of it and taking the steps to overcome it? These are the moments that confirm the value of what we as life planners can do. We can help make a real positive difference in people's lives. We can build and sustain excellent and satisfying relationships. We can be there for people every step of the way, through obstacles, learning, growth and change. We can experience the achievement of getting from here to there and help others do the same. We can live and help others live a more balanced, successful and joyful life by looking inside, embracing whatever change is necessary and staying motivated, engaged and disciplined enough to make the change permanent and meaningful. We can, and I hope that as a profession, we will.

Epilogue

For the last hundred-plus pages, we've been talking about looking inside—not just for the view, but to effectuate great things for yourself, your business and your clients. In so doing, you approach your life, practice and relationships with your clients in a way that aligns with your core values, dreams and goals. In short, you put your life *before* your business, and you bring matters of life into your financial planning business, so that you create happiness and success.

I am excited by the prospect that by reading this book and using it as a guide, you will be on the path to creating a better life and business. In creating more meaningful relationships with your clients, I hope they will be better able to change their lives in positive and meaningful ways as well.

We are not therapists, but we are financial diagnosticians. We are great listeners and are sensitive and aware of our clients' behaviors, actions and histories. Through listening, observing and utilizing the proper tools, we provide clients with the opportunity to look within themselves to find their truths, values and dreams. We hope and expect that their observations will lead to self-discovery and decisions that are productive, empowering, positive and affirming. We prescribe actions that we hope will bring clients closer to living their dreams. We back up our recommendations with sound financial judgment and advice that is based on research and experience. We stay with our clients every step of the way. For instance, I am still working with Dr. and Mrs. T. They still live in North Carolina. They are still struggling with their finances but have made progress, albeit very slowly. The jury's still out as to whether they will make it. I hope so.

Taking care of the business of life is a process with bumps, bruises, missteps and possibly even failure along the way. However, by breaking the process down into basic steps and keeping your focus on where you want and need to get to and why, it somehow becomes simpler. I applaud your courage, resolve and dedication to bringing the best of yourself forward. Yes, it requires resiliency and intention. Keep those qualities handy for ongoing reinforcement. We all need that!

I have benefited greatly, and continue to benefit, from the advice and support of other advisors and colleagues who have paved the way for this wonderful, exciting and fulfilling profession. I invite you to share your stories, successes, challenges and what you've learned with others around you. I also encourage you to participate in the forum on my website at *www.thebusinessoflife.net*. I want this to be a forum of learning for advisors striving beyond what has been prevalent up to today. I believe that together we can make a difference and change the landscape of what we offer to the world. I believe that by integrating this inside-out approach into your practice, you change for the better personally, improve your business, help your clients live a better life and make a positive contribution to society. What could be better than that?

Appendix

1. Individual Action Summary

2. Financial Satisfaction Survey

3. Wheel of Life Exercise

4. Money Memories Worksheet

5. Visualize Your Future Worksheet

6. Life Transition Survey

Appendix 1: Individual Action Summary

FINANCIAL FOCUS, LLC

Individual Action Summary

Client _____   Date _____

Assigned to: **Date due:**

_____ 1. _____ _____
              _____

_____ 2. _____ _____
              _____

_____ 3. _____ _____
              _____

_____ 4. _____ _____
              _____

_____ 5. _____ _____
              _____

_____ 6. _____ _____
              _____

_____ 7. _____ _____
              _____

_____ 8. _____ _____
              _____

_____ 9. _____ _____
              _____

_____ 10. _____ _____
              _____

Appendix 2: Financial Satisfaction Survey

Putting Money
in the **Context** of **Life**™

Financial Satisfaction Survey

Client Name _____   Date _____

Directions: *The statements below will help you to think about and assess how satisfied you are with many aspects of your financial life. Select and record your level of satisfaction for each statement.*

I am satisfied...	Not Satisfied 1	2	Moderately Satisfied 3	4	Very Satisfied 5
1...with my ability to meet my financial obligations.	☐	☐	☐	☐	☐
2...with the income my current job or career provides me.	☐	☐	☐	☐	☐
3...with my spending habits.	☐	☐	☐	☐	☐
4...with the level of debt I carry.	☐	☐	☐	☐	☐
5...with the "extras" that I am able to buy for myself and/or loved ones.	☐	☐	☐	☐	☐
6...with the level and quality of insurance protection I currently have.	☐	☐	☐	☐	☐
7...with the amount of money that I save and invest on a regular basis.	☐	☐	☐	☐	☐
8...with my current investment choices.	☐	☐	☐	☐	☐
9...that I am on track to build a sufficient retirement nest egg.	☐	☐	☐	☐	☐
10...with the level of employee benefits I receive.	☐	☐	☐	☐	☐
11...with my style of personal bookeeping and financial record management.	☐	☐	☐	☐	☐
1...ity to provide financial help t̶ ̶ers.	☐	☐	☐		

This Money Quotient tool is copyrighted and made available via licensing agreements — *www.moneyquotient.org.*

Appendix 3 – Wheel of Life Exercise

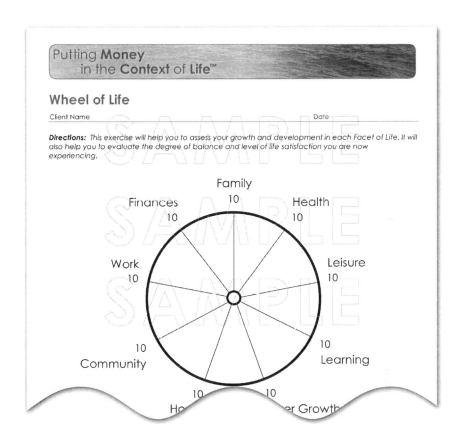

This Money Quotient tool is copyrighted and made available via licensing agreements — *www.moneyquotient.org*.

Appendix 4 – Money Memories Worksheet

Putting **Money** in the **Context** of **Life**™

Money Memories

Client Name _____ Date _____

Directions: Look for clues in your past that will help you to understand your current financial life. Starting with your childhood, what experiences have shaped your underlying beliefs and attitudes about money? What do your patterns of earning, saving, investing, and giving tell about you? Here is a list of questions to guide you in the reflection process.

1 What is your earliest money memory?

2 As a child, what was the most important lesson you learned about money?

3 Growing up in your family, was money mainly used to reward, punish, survive, impress, control, help others, have fun, buy love, reach goals, or _____?

4 What are the one-sentence messages regarding money that have stuck with you from your childhood? Where did you hear these messages?

5 What were the spending/saving patterns of your mother? Of your father?

6 Describe the work ethic of your mother and your father.

Appendix 5 – Life Transition Survey

Putting **Money** in the **Context** of **Life**™

Life Transitions Survey

Client Name _____ Date _____

Directions: *In each section, select the transitions that you are currently experiencing and those you are likely to experience in the future. In addition, check transitions in the short-term and long-term columns that you either hope to experience or anticipate with concern.*

Work Life Transitions	Currently experiencing	Anticipate short-term	Anticipate long-term
1 Change in career path	☐	☐	☐
2 New job	☐	☐	☐
3 Promotion	☐	☐	☐
4 Job loss	☐	☐	☐
5 Job restructure	☐	☐	☐
6 Education / retraining	☐	☐	☐
7 Sell or close business	☐	☐	☐
8 Transfer family business	☐	☐	☐
9 Gain a business partner	☐	☐	☐
10 Lose a business partner	☐	☐	☐
11 Downshift / simplify work life	☐	☐	☐
12 Sabbatical / leave of absence	☐	☐	☐
13 Start or purchase a business	☐	☐	☐
14 Retire	☐	☐	☐
15 Phase into retirement	☐	☐	☐
16 Other:	☐	☐	☐

...Transitions	Currently experiencing	Antici... ...	...ate
	☐		

This Money Quotient tool is copyrighted and made available via licensing agreements — *www.moneyquotient.org.*

Appendix 6 – Visualize Your Future Worksheet

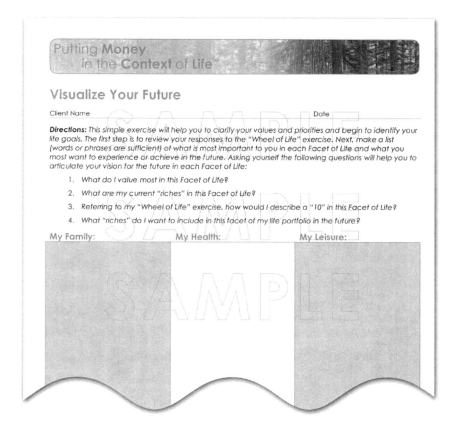

About the Author

Michael Kay, CFP®, is President of Financial Focus, LLC, a Registered Investment Advisory firm based in Livingston, NJ. A financial professional for over twenty-five years, Michael began his career as an accountant with a focus on tax, audit, financial accounting and forensic accounting. In 1985, he shifted his attention to personal financial planning, tax planning, investment strategy and wealth management as a Registered Representative of Securian Financial Services, Inc., until forming his own RIA in 2010.

Through the years, Michael has returned to academia as both student and teacher. In 2001, he earned a certificate of financial planning at New York University then returned in 2003 as an adjunct professor, teaching taxation in their CFP® Certification program.

Michael also studied with life planning pioneers Carol Anderson (Money Quotient) and George Kinder (The Kinder Institute of Life Planning). Inspired by what he learned, he explored and tested new methodologies, adopted those he considered to be the best and created a paradigm shift in his own practice.

Michael is a frequent presenter at Money Quotient trainings and retreats and is in demand as a speaker at industry events and public forums on financial planning. He is frequently quoted by the consumer media on issues related to personal finance, and serves as a resource for journalists who write for the financial planning industry. He is a regular blogger for both *PsychologyToday.com* and *Forbes.com*, and also writes a monthly column for *Advisorbiz.com*. In addition, Michael is a member of the Loring Ward Advisory Board and serves as the president of the Money Quotient Advisory Board.

You can learn more about Michael and Financial Focus at *www. financial-focus.net.*

Endnotes

[1] The term "Financial Life Planning" is a registered trademark of Money Quotient, Inc.

[2] Financial Life Planning® is a registered trademark of Money Quotient, Inc.

[3] Values-Based Financial Planning® is a registered trademark of Bill Bachrach.

[4] Copyright © 1986-2008, Certified Financial Planner Board of Standards Inc.

[5] Anderson C., "Life Planning," *Encyclopedia of Retirement and Finance*, Greenwood Press, 2003, p. 5.

[6] Anderson C., "Life Planning," *Encyclopedia of Retirement and Finance*, Greenwood Press, 2003, p. 2.

[7] Anderson C., Sharp D., "Research: Communications Issues in Life Planning: Defining Key Factors in Developing Successful Planner-Client Relationships," *Journal of Financial Planning*, FPA Press, Colorado, 2008, p. 4.

[8] Prochaska J.O. and Norcross J.C. and DiClemente C., *Changing for Good*, William Morrow and Co Inc., 1994, pp. 38-46.

[9] *CFP Certificant Manual*, Tab Practice Standards, page 10.05.

[10] Covey S.R., *The 7 Habits of Highly Effective People*, Free Press, New York, 1989, p. 287.

[11] Covey S.R., *The 7 Habits of Highly Effective People*, Free Press, New York, 1989, p. 95.

[12] Capacchione L., *Visioning Ten Steps to Designing The Life of Your Dreams*, Penguin Putnam Inc., New York, 2000, p. 199.

[13] Presentation materials: Coaching Course, Focus Four.

[14] Klontz T., Kahler R., and Klontz B., *The Financial Wisdom of Ebenezer Scrooge*, Health Communications Inc., p. 3.

[15] Kinder G., *Seven Stages of Money Maturity*, Dell, 1999, p. 147.

[16] Prochaska J.O., Norcross J.C., and DiClemente C., *Changing for Good*, William Morrow and Co Inc., 1994, p. 202.

Share the Financial Life Planning vision!

If this book has helped expand your perspective and you want to learn more about how to create and sustain the right business for you and your clients, we invite you to visit *The Business of Life* online. Michael Kay is continually developing new ways to work with clients and achieve greater levels of success. Watch for new books and other inspirational materials.

We would also like to hear from you! Share your insights and questions with Michael and other professionals by commenting online. Join the conversation and contribute to the great meeting of financial minds on the *TheBusinessofLife.net*.

If you hear Michael speak at industry conferences, please be sure to introduce yourself and strike up a conversation. You can also invite Michael to speak to your professional group. If you'd like to provide colleagues with copies of this book, volume discounts are available from the publisher.

Visit TheBusinessofLife.net for more information.

FINANCIAL FOCUS, LLC
Life Planning – Wealth Management

Transforming vision into reality

We welcome inquiries from advisors who might be interested in adopting the Financial Focus philosophy and/or brand.

Financial Focus, LLC
70 South Orange Avenue, Suite 245
Livingston, NJ 07039
Phone: (973) 533-0666 • Fax: (973) 533-6460
www.financial-focus.net

Breinigsville, PA USA
22 November 2010
249802BV00002B/1/P